7:17

A Memoir by: Rayna Gray

Printed in the United States of America

Publishing services by Arnaz Publishing, PA.

ISBN: 9780985737351

Library of Congress Control Number: 2012955503

My Dedication...

I dedicate this book to God. I thank you for providing me with the words needed to fill the pages of this book. I thank you for never leaving my side or forsaking me; especially when I knew I had fallen astray and had let go of your unchanging hands. Thank you for the many lessons that I had to endure in my life in order to find my purpose and be obedient to your will. I know without those challenges I would not be connected to your strength, which picked me up from rock bottom and gave me the will to see the truth. You are the guiding light in my life and I am honored to serve you Lord. It gives me great pleasure to be submissive to your word. I know you love me and I am happy to know that you are not done with me.

2 Chronicles 7:17-18 New International Version

> **17**"As for you, if you walk before me faithfully as David your father did, and do all I command, and observe my decrees and laws, **18** I will establish your royal throne, as I covenanted with David your father when I said, 'You shall never fail to have a successor to rule over Israel.'

Acknowledgements

I give all thanks and glory to God. Because of you I exist. I made it through and I have persevered. You have always known the plan and the route that I must take in order to be in tune with your ultimate purpose, and I thank you. I mention you first because I know the power of your love. I have not only been blessed to feel your compassion and to receive the many blessings you have bestowed upon me, but I witness your greatness each day as I live my life through giving and educating women and men about domestic violence.

I send a very special thank you to the love of my life- my wonderful husband Wallace (Duke) - for being my biggest cheerleader. No matter the dream or the size of the project I pitch to you, you always stand beside me and you love me for exactly who I am.

To my children, Wallace Jr., Ryan, Ryir, Rymir and Rylei, I am blessed to call you my sons. Make your mark on this world because God created you for excellence and nothing less than that.

I thank my mothers, for whom God has blessed me with two; my biological mother, Judith, and my Aunt, Deborah-who I call my mom- who raised me. Judith, despite the obstacles you've faced, you have made it through. When I look at you I am strengthened. You are truly an example of a walking testimony.

Deborah, you introduced me to Christ and you've prayed for me every day and every night. You believed in me when I didn't believe in myself. Thank you for taking us in and for caring for us when no one else would.

I thank all of my siblings- Gary, Fred, Eugene (I miss you so much), Vaughn, Kimberly, Kenya, Titus, Nichole, Shelita, Glen, Akea and Chantel; I have learned so much from each and every one of you. All of you are going through this life journey with me and I appreciate you. I love you all.

Uncle Irving, Uncle Mike, Uncle Clayton, and Uncle Larry, you each have impacted my life in different ways and have taught me many valuable life lessons. I love you guys.

To the best mother-in-law, Yvonne, and father-in-law, Dwain, thank you for loving me and being there for my family. You helped me take care of Ryir when I needed it the most and I could never repay you for your kindness. You also produced amazing children who treat me like I'm one of the family. My sisters-in-law, La' Kisha, Nakia, Felicia, Dionna and my brothers-in-law, Tyrek, Troy, Jason, and Keith, I thank you for the sibling love.

I say a special thank you to Shelita Jackson for being more than just a friend. You pushed me when I needed it and you see things in me that I don't see within myself. I also thank you for the help with editing this book.

Last but never least; I thank all of my family and friends for their genuine love and support. I thank all whom have crossed my path and had an impact on my life; may it be positive or negative-it has all helped with my growth. Continue to pray for me and know that each day I am living with purpose.

Contents

Prologue

On July 17, 1978 I was born into this world. When I think back to my childhood there are many memories that I cannot recall; specifically the good ones. I've tried often to recall the scent of the first flower I smelled, or the taste of my first piece of candy and the excitement that I must have had because I love candy; but I always draw a blank. It's as if my life did not begin until the year of 1989.

I am the fifth child of my mother's seven offspring, and the only child that does not share a father with my siblings. I have two sisters, Toya and Dominique, and four brothers, Kevin, Stephen, Victor and Benjamin. My mother told me I was born in a housing project in South Philadelphia, but the first house I can remember living in was located at 5027 Green Street- in the Germantown section of Philadelphia. My father, whose name is James, was an active parent in my life for eleven years; but even with that information I had been given I am not sure what happened to eleven years of my memories Maybe I blocked them out because things were not pleasant or perhaps I have a really bad memory. Either way it's puzzling to me that there is a fog around that era of my life.

My first life changing memory that I was able to pull from the fog brought me back to December 18, 1985.

At that time I was a petite seven year old girl. My Aunt Dee and Uncle Tommy had come over to our house in the evening. There was a sense of urgency regarding their visit so my mother told all the children to leave the room so the adults could talk.

Aunt Dee delivered the heart wrenching news that their baby sister, Shingie, was murdered by her boyfriend. He had stabbed her in the heart during a violent and very physical fight. He was known to be abusive towards my Aunt Shingie and she was the first woman I knew of who had been a victim of domestic violence. With her passing, two beautiful young daughters were snatched from their mother-and her one daughter, who was only five months old at the time of her murder-was fathered by the man who had killed her.

I can vividly remember the screams of my mother. They penetrated through my soul and I felt as if I had been sitting in the room with the adults when the news was given. No one and nothing could calm my mother down. She continued to scream out as her pain turned to rage, and then to disbelief, and then back to agony. That day changed our lives forever.

The day of my aunt's funeral we were not allowed to attend. My mother said we were too young but we still wanted to go. I saw everyone in their black and I wanted to mourn as well. I wanted to see my Aunt Shingie one last time. However, my mother was firm in her decision that we would stay at home.

A few days after my aunt's funeral, I was asleep in the back bedroom with my oldest and youngest sisters, Toya and Dominique. Toya slept on a twin mattress across from the bunk beds Dominique and I shared. While on the bottom bunk I was awakened to an extremely bright light. I could never fully verbally characterize the strength and color of that light but it indescribably illuminated my bedroom. It was almost as if the sun was sitting inside of my room, blinding me, yet pulling me closer to its powerful illumination.

When I opened my eyes and looked up at the bedpost, Aunt Shingie was standing at my bed. I couldn't believe it! I was a young child but I could clearly see her. She was beautiful; dressed in all white, with a radiant glow that surrounded her body. Her hair was curled to the back, just like I had remembered her wearing her hair, and her skin was flawless. She was an angel!

She looked down at me and initially I pulled the covers over my face because I was frightened. I had never experienced seeing a vision, let alone my aunt in the spirit form and it was overwhelming. While I was under the covers I kept thinking I had to be dreaming; but I was not. This was the real deal.

I slowly pulled the covers down my face and stopped right when they got above my nose. Then I slowly turned my head towards Toya's bed. I wanted to see if she was awake and I would have felt less afraid if she was, but the only people up were me and my Aunt Shingie. She was looking directly at me and I froze. Our eyes locked upon each other and I began to feel safe as the love in her eyes warmed my heart. She was not here to hurt me. She was love. But as fast as I began to become comfortable with her presence, she disappeared.

I screamed out loud, waking everyone in the house, including my mother. I shared with them my experience and everyone believed me but we never really talked about it after that night. My experience was unclear to me for many years. I never knew why she had chosen to visit me but it became clear later on in life. Aunt Shingie was my protector. She had come to me to remind me of how she had lost her life. She didn't want me to fear her but to learn from the pains she had endured. I could only say I wished I had understood her message sooner but my life was not wired that way. Throughout my life she would revisit me. Seeing her brought a warning or much needed protection. My aunt knew how much I needed her and nineteen years from the day I had first saw her vision, she would be with me a time in my life when I needed to remember her most.

Chapter 1
In the Beginning

The very first time my Aunt Shingie helped me was the following summer after she had passed away. Dominique, Victor, and I were watching television in the boy's bedroom. We lived in a three bedroom house but we did not share the same amenities throughout our home. My brothers had a television in their bedroom and my sisters and I had the cooling system-which was a basic box fan- in our room. When we wanted to watch television we would bring our fan into their room. Dominique was usually appointed the fan-carrier and was always asked to do things by my brother Victor. Now, although I was two years older than Dominique, she just did everything better and faster than I did. She learned how to jump rope, braid hair, and tie her shoes before I could. When something needed to be done my family would call upon Dominique and I hated that.

So as usual, Victor asked Dominique to go into our room and bring back the fan. She hopped up and went into our bedroom to retrieve it, but when she returned she was empty handed. She could not unplug it. This brought me great excitement because this was my opportunity to show Dominique and my family that I could do something she couldn't.

Victor looked at me and said, "Do you think you can get it?" I didn't respond. I leapt up from the floor and ran into our bedroom. I was filled with as much confidence as a seven year old could have and I tried to pull the cord out of the wall. I used all the strength I had within me but the cord was not budging. I pulled at it again. I tugged on it but it would not move. It was like it had been glued into the socket. However, I was determined to get the fan unplugged because I had to prove to Dominique and Victor that I was good at something.

When I had grew tired of tugging at the cord I opted for plan-b. I found the middle of the cord and I folded the white cord at the middle, and then I put it in my mouth and bit down on it. Immediately my body began to convulse uncontrollably. Hundreds of colors were racing past my eyes and I could see my own skeleton. I felt my body begin to shut down and it was at that time I remembered my Aunt Shingie. I thought to myself, while my teeth were locked on the cord, "Please Aunt Shingie don't let me die!"

As soon as that thought had ended the cord fell from out of my mouth. I darted into my mother's room. My mother, my stepdad Tony, and my mother's friend, Mildred, were sitting in the smoke filled room that reeked of marijuana. My face had begun to swell and my mother started yelling and cussing at the same time when I ran towards her.

"Rayna, what the h**l happened to you!" My mouth was severely swollen so she could barely understand me when I muffled, "I bit on the cord." Dominique and Victor rushed into the room and told my mother how I was trying to get the fan unplugged. Tony began to yell at Victor for sending me to get the fan, and although it was clearly not his fault, he continued to apologize as my mother and I crawled into the ambulance as we headed to Temple University Hospital.

After the doctor had examined me, he stated the

inside of my mouth was burnt badly and that the structure of the left side of my mouth had been pulled to the right side. My face was disfigured. The doctor informed my mother that if the cord had been in my mouth a second longer I would have died. He noticed my mother starring at the humongous scar that began to appear on my face and he said, "That will heal. It will shrink but it needs time." My mother seemed relieved to know that I would not look deformed forever and then he added, "She's going to miss the rest of the school semester. She'll need to recover at home and the pain she'll endure will be best treated if she completes her schooling at home. Not to mention kids can be cruel and they will surely tease her for the way her face looks now."

This news upset me extremely because this was my second time completing the first grade. I was now doing well and didn't want to miss any days of school. I was not a child that did not enjoy school. I had only failed the previous year because I could not see. I went the entire school year unable to see the black board. I could never understand the delay in getting my eyes tested but there was a need for me to be seen by an eye doctor. My mother had finally taken me to see an ophthalmologist and they learned I was legally blind and had to wear bifocals.

To calm my apparent worries about missing school, my mother promised me she would get my schoolwork. She assured me things would work out because there were only two months left in the school calendar.

The following day we had to visit a burn center to see if I had suffered internal damage. Luckily, there was none. Following that visit my mother took me to see my father. My father played a very important role in my life. Although he and my mother were no longer together, he did not let that interfere with how well he took care of me. Every weekend he would pick me up, he brought me clothes and a few toys, but most importantly he loved me. I can remember him telling me to cut out any toys I had liked out of the newspaper's advertisements and when I gave them to him, he'd always get the toys I wanted. I loved my dad with all of my heart. He showed his little girl what love felt like and it was a feeling I never wanted to end.

When my dad saw my face he was very upset. He did not like what he saw but he looked at me and said, "You are my baby girl. You're pretty no matter what." His words were reassuring and I trusted my dad. I knew if he said I was beautiful and that my scars would heal, then that's what would happen. The injuries I received from the electric cord healed and the only scar that I have today is barely visible. It sits at the left corner of my mouth and you'd have to stare at me intensely to see the flaw.

So Aunt Shingie had come to my rescue once, but within a month after my first accident, she was back. I was playing outside with two little girls that were sisters, who lived a block away from me. On this particular day my mother and Mildred were sitting on the porch talking. Out of nowhere a dog appeared and started to chase me. In the eyes of this frightened eight year old, the dog was gigantic, with large dark eyes, oversized teeth, and he looked evil. I tried to run as fast as I could to get away from the dog, while my mother and Mildred kept yelling for me to stop running. I could not stop. I didn't want the dog to eat me alive.

As I ran I shouted out loudly, "Aunt Shingie please don't let this dog kill me!" When I got to the edge of my street and readied myself to keep going, I turned back to see where the dog was but he was no longer directly behind me. The dog had been hit by an approaching car. My mother ran and picked me up. She could not believe what she had just witnessed.

As a little girl I didn't know who God was but I knew that some kind of way Aunt Shingie, or what appeared to be Aunt Shingie, could help me. I now know that God sent the vision of Aunt Shingie to get me out of life threatening incidents because I did not know how to call upon him. At an early age I was called on and protected by God. I had work to do and my time on earth would not be cut short until I had fulfilled my purpose.

A few years later we moved to North Philadelphia to a much smaller house. Tony worked for the United States Postal Service and my mother was a stay at home mom. Frequently my mother would go to the bar and hang out with her friends, but when we moved it seemed as if it became a daily event. There was a woman named Ms. Tiny who lived around the corner from us with her four children, and she and my mother became bar buddies.

Days would pass when we didn't see our mother. It became a normal occurrence for her not to be in our home. Tony would have to feed us and get us ready for school, and the more time my mother spent outside of the home, the more things in our home began to disappear. All types of household items suddenly crept away, like our clocks, radios, pictures, and anything that could be sold for some petty cash.

Tony and my mother began to argue whenever she was in the house. He had grown tired of her ways and bluntly accused her of using drugs. His accusations were far from being farfetched because my mother had become addicted to crack cocaine.

The relationship between Tony and my mother got worse as her addiction grew and she would go missing for weeks at a time. Tony's frustration had boiled over and one day when she came home, Tony packed his things and left. He didn't take Dominique and Benjamin, who are his biological children.

At this time a lot of changes in the household had occurred. My mother was on drugs and Tony had gone. My brothers Kevin and Stephen were in Delaware- in a program called job corps- Toya was pregnant by a man who was twenty-four and she was only fifteen years old, and Victor was living with friends while working at a pizza store. Our food supply was really low because money was not coming into the house, and the money that would come in from our state allotted assistance check, went to crack instead of groceries. Toya's small food vouchers from the Women, Infant, and Children (WIC) Program helped keep cereal and milk in our refrigerator and when he could, Victor would bring food home from the pizzeria. While home on a weekend pass from his job corps program, Stephen was at home with us watching television. I walked down the street to a neighbor's house named Mr. Frank to see if my mother was there. She had been gone for several weeks and I wanted her to know Stephen was home.

Mr. Frank was an older gentleman that had become friends with my mother. I knocked on his door and he opened it; just like he had done any other time I went looking for my mother. I asked, "Mr. Frank is my mother here," and without answering my questions he replied, "Come on in."

I rushed over to the coffee table to play with the many animal figurines. He kept the table full of toys and since I didn't have many toys I always enjoyed playing with the animals. Mr. Frank interrupted my play time when he called me over to him. He picked me up and sat me on his lap. I was afraid and uncomfortable because this had never happened before. I asked him where my mother was and he said, "She'll be here shortly." He then asked me for a hug and held me so tightly that I could barely move. I tried to wiggle out of his grip and then he lifted up my skirt and placed his fingers inside of my vagina. I started to scream as loud as I could and instantly he let me go.

I ran out of his house and straight back home. When I got in the house I told Toya and Stephen what had just happened and they went to Mr. Frank's house. They rung the bell and banged on his door but he did not answer. They didn't call the cops. Instead the decision was made to tell my mother and see how she wanted to handle it. When my mother finally came home we told her how Mr. Frank had stuck his hands into my vagina and made me sit on his lap. My mother said, "He was just drunk. He's an old man but he won't do that again."

The cops were not called and my mother did not condemn Mr. Frank. He supported my mother's drug habit and she was not about to lose his support by having that dirty old man arrested. So nothing was ever done. Life continued how it had been going and in November of 1988, Toya delivered my nephew, Marcus. Our living arrangements were deplorable and she did not want to have a newborn baby living in squalor, so Toya moved in with our Aunt Dee in Mount Airy. Dominique, Benjamin, and I were left to fend for ourselves. At the age of ten I was now the primary caregiver and I was determined to take care of my little brother and sister.

My mother's addiction was beyond out of control. We did not have heat, hot water, food or clean clothes; and finding my mother was often a task that we had given up on. One of the neighbors across the street intervened by inviting us to church. I had no clue what church was, because we had never went before, but I was happy to go because of the chicken dinner we ate after each service. During the school week I had to get Dominique and Benjamin up for school, bathe them in cold water, and often I had to clean Benjamin's bed because he peed in it continuously. I had to make sure we were up on time because if we were late we would miss the free breakfast that the school provided; and that just wasn't an option for us. We needed all the food we could get. We were teased daily at school because despite my best efforts to wash the pee smell off of our bodies, it stayed on us. The odor was just too strong and without hot water and detergent, or sometimes soap, my best efforts didn't cut it. Our clothes were always dirty and our hair was never maintained. At times school was dreadful but I loved being there. Not only for the free meals but because I loved to learn.

I began to think of ways to earn extra money to help us eat. We needed food and when Victor couldn't drop us off a few cold pizzas, I had to hustle. At school there was a boy named Harry who I sat next to. He paid me fifty cents whenever I cleaned out his desk. Then once we got home I'd knock on as many neighbors' doors as I could to see if they needed me to go to the store for them. They must of knew we were in bad shape because no one ever told me no.

I used whatever money I earned to buy chicken wings from the Chinese store, fried rice, or rice and gravy. Whatever was the cheapest meal was what we had to eat. There were three of us and our options were very limited. When I went to the corner store, there was a woman employee who would always give us extra food whenever we shopped there. Everyone knew that our mother was on drugs and that we were fending for ourselves.

My mother's disappearance had quite an effect on me because I don't remember what she looked like as a child. For that time period she is just a dark figure in my memory bank. I barely saw her and without a picture I could not say I knew her face back then.

When Thanksgiving rolled around that year we visited with my Aunt Dee. While we were at her home she made sure we had clean clothing and she fed us well. I loved being at her home. It was like being in paradise. The cabinets and refrigerator were stocked with food. The neighborhood was beautiful and we were able to be carefree as we played outside or indoors with toys. I was having the time of my young life.

Aunt Dee had three children of her own, Phillip, Christine and Timothy; and she had taken my little cousins Ashley and Amber in when Aunt Shingie was murdered. She was very loving to her children and us as well. I loved it over there and I didn't want to leave, but I knew the end of our stay was fast approaching. When Sunday came it was clear it was time for us to go but before we went back home Aunt Dee wrote her telephone number on a piece of paper and said, "If anything happens you make sure you call me." I promised her I would and we headed back to our home; the place that I dreaded.

Spring sprung into the air but our situation didn't change much. The weather was warmer so it wasn't as cold as it was in our home, but we were still dingy and hungry-and without our mother. While in school one day my teacher's classroom phone rang. When she hung up she told me to go to the office because I was getting an early dismissal. When I arrived at the office Victor, Dominique and Benjamin were waiting for me. Seeing my siblings at my school prompted me to ask them, "What's going on?" Victor looked at me and said, "The house is boarded up." I didn't fully understand what boarded up meant but I knew that we were homeless.

For some time Tony had stopped paying the mortgage and the bank came to claim their property. Victor took us back to our house, where my mother was waiting in the backyard. She looked at me and said, "Climb in that window and get us some clothes." I rolled my eyes at her. How dare she ask me to do such a thing? We were homeless and I had barely seen her and now she wanted me to break into our house.

I climbed into the window but I did not follow her instructions. I brought out my Kit and Caboodle doll, along with the horse my father bought for me. I was angry at my mother and I didn't want to help her. She yelled at me but I didn't care. When we finally got the things from out of the house that she wanted, we walked around the front of the house and went down the street to move in with Mr. Frank. I couldn't believe it. How could my mother trust him after what he had done to me? Why would she betray me by moving us in with a known pervert?

The first night at Mr. Frank's house was extremely scary. After sitting upstairs in a back bedroom for a while, I got hungry and wanted to see what my mother had cooked for us. I went downstairs to find raw floured chicken sitting on the table, but my mother was not in the kitchen. She left and I did not see her again until years later.

When I saw that my mother was gone I sat Dominique and Benjamin down and explained to them how things were going to be during our stay at Mr. Frank's. We would all sleep in the back bedroom, we would travel to the bathroom together, and no one was allowed to be in Mr. Frank's bedroom or alone with him for any reason. I did not want what happened to me to happen to my brother or sister.

Our routine didn't change. I bathed, fed and clothed my sister and brother. When we were not barricaded in the bedroom, I followed them everywhere they needed to go in Mr. Frank's house. He tolerated us and didn't say much too either one of us. This living arrangement went on for quite some time until at school I received another message from my teacher to head to the office.

Waiting for me at the office was Victor, Dominique, Benjamin, and a woman whose name I cannot remember. I do remember her saying that she worked for the Department of Human Services. In a very sarcastic voice I asked, "Why are we getting out of school early?" She ignored my sassiness and said, "You've been at your neighbor's house too long. Your mother has abandoned you and we have to take you into foster care." I was shocked. I asked, "Are you taking us to the same place," and she responded, "No. Unfortunately we do not have a place where all of you can go together. We will have to separate you."

That day I knew what it was like to have resentment towards another person. I hated my mother. She had left us and now I would be taken away from my siblings. Through my tears I tried to explain to the social worker that my father did not live that far from the school and that his house was right around the corner. She told me that without an address she could not take us there. At this time my father and I had grown apart. Since my mother's drug abuse had taken a turn for the worse, I had only seen him once.

The woman took us back to Mr. Frank's house to get our clothes. While she helped us put what little items we had in bags, I remembered what my Aunt Dee had told me. I found her number and told the lady that I had somewhere for us to go. I called Aunt Dee and explained to her what was going on, and she asked to speak with the social worker.

The social worker told my aunt that a report had been made by a neighbor that we were abandoned by our mother, and since she had not seen my mother, nor could she contact her, we'd have to be placed into a foster home. Then I heard the lady say, "Okay, all three of them," as she pulled out a notepad and wrote down my aunt's address. She then handed me the phone and when I said hello my aunt said, "Everything is going to be okay. Y'all are going to come and stay with me. Just listen to her and I'll see you shortly."

Chapter 2
Saved

It was towards the end of May in 1989, when we arrived at my aunt's house in Mount Airy. My aunt took me into the kitchen and sat me down. She reiterated to me that we had nothing to worry about and we would be taken care of. She warmly hugged me and looked into my eyes and said, "You'll be able to be a child again. You do not have to worry about taking care of your siblings anymore. I can do that now." What a sense of relief and happiness I felt. For two years I had been struggling to give all I had to my sister and brother, and now we finally had some assistance.

My aunt jumped right into provider and protector mode. She discarded all of our clothes, which smelled horrid and were so worn they were unable to be resurrected. I had to be taken to the dentist. Due to lack of dental care my gums covered the majority of my teeth, and it was hard for me to eat without being in excruciating pain. My aunt was on her job. However, navigating the different systems for us was difficult for her because she was not our biological mother; nor did she have legal guardianship. Nonetheless, by God's grace she was able to get it done. She got us health insurance and enrolled us into school. We had endless doctor's appointments because we had not been seen by one in so many years. Moving with my aunt was the best thing that could have happen to us. My aunt was a single mother raising ten children-only three being her biological children- but she still made sure we all had everything we needed, especially love.

The date of June 4th came and it was a significant day for me. On that date my Aunt Shingie was born and it was the day I accepted Jesus Christ as my personal Lord and Savior. I will never forget that day. Aunt Dee took us into the living room and explained Jesus Christ's purpose. She told us how he died on the cross for our sins and how on the third day, after his death, he arose with all power in his hands. With such comfort and certainty she further enlightened us about all of his goodness and mercy. She had us repeat the sinner's prayer and told us that we were saved. It was the best feeling ever because by this time I began to develop an understanding of Jesus Christ and his almighty father God. I began to understand that it was he who had saved me and that was amazing!

Church was like our new home because we went there a lot. When people in the church and the neighborhood asked Aunt Dee who we were, she replied, "My children." She never referred to us as her nieces and nephews. So it was a natural occurrence for us to refer to her as, mom, even though I can't pinpoint the day or time when the name transition occurred. It felt so good to call her mom. All the children in my aunt's household became brothers and sisters; no longer did we refer to each other as cousins. We stuck by each other, stood up for one another, and we were all very close.

My mom did everything for us and she never made me feel like an outsider. The bond she and I shared was extremely close. We talked about everything. I can remember giving her pedicures and cleaning her room up just to make her happy; because she made me so happy. I loved her with my whole heart.

Besides our active church involvement, education was another important factor in our household. I did well in school and when I was accepted into a special academic admittance program in middle school, my mom was very proud of me. I did my best to please her.

When I was in the eighth grade Toya ran into our stepfather Tony on the bus; prompting him to return into our lives. Benjamin was having a difficult time living with my mom because whenever our biological mother called she continued to feed him promises of an immediate reunion and of better days as a complete family. He had believed her. He held onto her words but when it was clear her pledges would never come true, he began to act out.

With Tony back in the picture, Benjamin moved in with him. Dominique and I would go over Tony's house on the weekends to visit; even though we really didn't want to because we did not like his girlfriend. She was mean to us and eventually I stopped going.

A few months had passed and we were sitting at the dining room table doing our homework. The phone rang and my mom answered it. I knew from the look that grew on her face that something was terribly wrong. When she hung up she told us that Tony was in the hospital in Washington D.C. He had cancer. He was a veteran and the D.C. hospital he was in was the best at treating the form of cancer he had. Dominique and I began to cry and asked if we could go and see him. My mom didn't want us to see him in the deteriorated shape his girlfriend told her he was in. A week later we got the dreaded call. Tony was dead.

His funeral was going to be in Boston, that's where he was from. My biological mother knew Tony had passed and she wanted to take us to the funeral. My

mom was hesitant but eventually gave her the permission to take us. Before we left, my mom talked to Dominique and I about being safe. We hadn't seen my mother in over three years and she wanted us to pay careful attention to her actions. We had been instructed to call her if anything seemed strange or inappropriate.
Dominique, Benjamin, our mother and I boarded a train headed to Boston to bury her husband. When we arrived in Boston, Tony's family and friends welcomed us with open arms. They gave us money and gifts. I was treated as if I was Tony's biological child.

The day of the funeral arrived and I was very nervous. I had never been to a funeral before. While sitting through the service I became very emotional. I could not believe Tony was gone. Although I was his step-daughter, he always treated me like one of his own children. I loved Tony. I began to yell and cry hysterically when I laid my eyes on Tony's corpse. He did not look like himself. All of his hair was gone because of the cancer treatments and he was frail. Through my crying eyes I swore I saw him breathing, but surely he was deceased. I hated every minute of that funeral.

The day after the funeral I called my mom to let her know we were on our way back to Philadelphia. She instructed me to call her as soon as we got in the city so Toya could meet us and bring us home. My mom had to stay with the children so Toya would pick us up. We arrived in Philadelphia very late that evening. When we got back my mother had other plans for us. She took us to Mr. Frank's house. I could not believe it! Nothing had changed with her.

I took Dominique and Benjamin up to the back bedroom and called my mom. I told her where we were and she was irate. It was too late in the evening for her to send Toya for us, so my mom prayed for our safety over the phone. She told me not to leave the room until Toya got there in the morning. Knowing my mother was still a drug addict, I told Dominique and Benjamin to hide their money under their pillows before they fell asleep so our mother wouldn't steal it. But when we woke up all the money and gifts we received were gone...and so was our mother. I didn't see my mother for a few years after that incident.

Life continued as usual after we returned to my mom's house. Benjamin returned to live with us and he started to misbehave again. He was disruptive in school and at home. The absence and broken promises made by our mother, along with the death of his father, took a toll on him.

Shortly after Tony's death my mom received another call that would change the dynamics of my family forever. Tony had a will and in it he stated that he wanted his children to live with his cousin, who resided in New Hampshire. My mom did her best to explain to us what this all meant, and without legal guardianship Dominique and Benjamin moved to New Hampshire.

This was a very sad time for me because it felt like I was losing a part of me. I was their big sister, their protector, and suddenly they were leaving me. Now the only people living in my mom's house were Christine-and her three children-Phillip, Timothy, Toya, Marcus-Toya's son-Ashley, Amber and I. There was emptiness when Dominique and Benjamin left and that void was never filled.
A few years had passed without any drama. Toya and Marcus moved. She moved in with her boyfriend and she had a little girl named Rachel with him. Phillip moved into an apartment, Timothy moved with friends, and Ashley moved in with her father. Amber, Christine-her children- and I were the only ones living at home with my mom.

It was around this time I started to like boys but my mom wouldn't allow me to date. I attended The

Philadelphia High School for Girls, which was classified as one of the best high schools in Philadelphia. I also started working. I had an after school job at a daycare, where I made sixty dollars a week. It wasn't a lot of money but it was enough for me to get my hair done and a few necessities.

I was a teenager so my mom began to let me have a little freedom, because overall I was a good girl. I was a good student, I did what she asked, and I helped out with Amber while she worked. On the weekends I attended house parties with my friend, Mena, who was dating Timothy. I started to gain confidence in myself and paid more attention to my appearance; because I began to get noticed by boys. A friend of Mena's named Jay took notice and he and I began to talk. I didn't tell my mom about him because she would have killed me.

Jay didn't live too far from the daycare, so after work I would sneak and see him. I would go over his house and I felt very special when I got to meet his family. I was fifteen and he was seventeen. He was way more experienced than I was, and that showed when he brought up conversations about sex. I wasn't thinking about sex. I didn't want to have sex, but the more he talked about it the more I wanted him to like me. I didn't want to appear immature so eventually I gave in. I regretted my decision shortly afterwards.

Our family moved out of Mount Airy into a bigger house in West Oak Lane. In this house I had my own room. This was the first time in my life that I ever had my own room. It was pink and I loved it. Being the new girl on the block I began to catch the eyes of some of the neighborhood boys. One in particular kept his focus on me, his name was David. He was nineteen and he seriously pursued me, even though I told him I was seeing someone else. He just didn't care. He would come over my house and sit on the steps with me, and we'd talk all night. By this time Jay was selling drugs and didn't have much time for me, so I didn't see him that often.

One day while I was sitting on the steps with David my cordless phone rang. When I answered, it was Jay. I told David who was on the phone...what a mistake. David started to talk loudly, hoping to be heard. Of course Jay heard him and immediately he began to question me. I was scared and nervous. The call ended with him hanging up on me, but not before he dumped me. David came to my rescue telling me it was going to be okay and that I didn't need to be with someone who sold drugs anyway.

That day David and I began dating. I did things with David that Jay and I never did. We went out to eat, to the mall, and to the movies. David was already out of high school and working at a man's clothing store. He would meet me after school and walk me home. David met my mom and she liked him. We were always together. David lived around the corner from me with a few of his friends. I began to hang out there all the time. When I met his friend's girlfriends, I felt very strange because I was much younger than them. Young and all I still did the one thing that they were all doing...and that was having sex. At that young age I got nothing out of it. I began to believe that sex was made for men because I didn't get any satisfaction. I remember David asking me if I was on birth control. When I said I wasn't, he said we would use condoms. But when I expressed to him that I didn't understand what I was supposed to feel when we had sex, he suggested we stop using condoms. We did, but still I got nothing out of it. I was too young to understand it.

My mom knew that I had become sexually active. It's like they say, "A mother knows when her child is having sex." We never talked about sex or birth control, but she told me not to get pregnant. I think she believed that if she got me birth control she would be encouraging me to have sex, so she didn't take me to the doctor's to get any. She was a devout Christian and sex before marriage was something she did not condone.

David wanted me to get on birth control but I was scared to. I didn't have my mom's consent and I didn't want to sneak and go to a free clinic. I needed her help but my mom wasn't going to back me on my decision to have premarital sex. The thought of disappointing her sickened me but it didn't stop me from sleeping with Jay or David. I guess a part of me thought I wasn't going to get pregnant...well I did. I was sixteen years old and with child, and I didn't have to tell my mom I was expecting because she already knew. When I told David I was pregnant he made plans for me to get an abortion.

One night while lying in my bed I began to get awful pains in my stomach. My mom rushed me to the emergency room. The doctor said I had pain because my body was trying to adjust to the pregnancy. That night in the hospital room my mom looked me and said, "You're not getting an abortion. Fornication is a sin but the conception of your baby is not. " I was going to have my baby, she settled that for me. She made me believe that I could continue my educational plans and become a pediatrician. That night a heavy load was lifted off of my shoulders because I knew I had the support of my mom, and that she would never leave my side. She loved me no matter what stupid mistakes I had made and I needed her in my life.

My pregnancy was tough. I lost my job because I kept falling asleep at work. My grades slipped and I was tired most of the time. David and I ended our relationship because we could not get along. I barely saw him and when I did, we argued. I could remember feeling like I hated him. There was nothing we could agree upon, not even a name for our child. He was obsessed with me having a girl and the day we went into the doctor's office to find out the gender, he quickly became irate.

The doctor said, "Congratulations, you're having a boy!" That was all David needed to hear to ruin my office visit. David began to act like a jerk and kept saying sarcastic remarks. I couldn't wait to leave. When I got home I told Christine and Phillip I was having a boy. Phillip suggested I name him Ryan, because my name is Rayna; so there was a similarity. Christine suggested Avery as a middle name because Ivory is my middle name, so with their help I named my son Ryan Avery Norris.

During the third trimester of my pregnancy the living arrangements inside of my home changed again. My mom left her home and moved into an apartment with Amber. She allowed Christine to keep the house. My mom never said why she moved but it was clear to me that she was tired. She had raised so many kids that she needed a break, and her own space. She had helped Christine with her children and she had done all she could do to help me; so I wasn't hurt when she moved out. I made the decision to move in with Phillip into a small apartment in the Spring Garden section of the city. I am not sure why but I wanted to be with him.

Ryan's due-date was August 11, 1995, but I began having contractions on July 30th. The week where my contractions were gradually increasing, I moved back in with Christine. She lived closer to the hospital and I wanted to be around someone who could help me if my water broke. During the course of that week I went to the hospital several times, but the doctors kept sending me home. I was having plenty of pain but had not dilated a centimeter. Everyone suggested I walk if I wanted the baby to hurry up and come on out, and so I walked as much as I could.

There was an active heat wave in the city but I still walked. I was so ready to meet Ryan so I walked up and down the block, around the corner, down the street, up and down steps, and then I started my routine from the top. While all this was going on I had not heard from David.

On August 3rd, my mom came to visit me. She took me back to the hospital because she could see I could no longer bare the discomfort. I was in so much pain that I was terrified. When we arrived my doctor was called and he rushed to the hospital. My mom and Christine kept trying to calm me down but I could not take the pain. I was screaming and hollering. My seventeen year old body and mind could not handle labor pains. I needed something to take the pain away. They gave me Demerol, a medication which was supposed to help with the pain, but it gave me an allergic reaction instead. My lips broke out in hives but I really didn't care because the pain had subsided.

When the doctor finally arrived I was completely out of it. I could not comprehend or even push for that matter. I was so weak that the doctor had to use forceps to pull Ryan out. Ryan arrived in this world on August 4, 1995, at 9:00 a.m. I remember the talk show Jenny Jones was playing on the television in the background. David, not surprisingly, missed the birth of his son because I could not locate him. Later that day, he had gotten word that I was in the hospital and he came to meet Ryan. When he arrived and found out that I had already completed the paperwork for Ryan's birth certificate, he was furious. I had named our son and there was no changing it- at least that's what I told him.

After leaving the hospital, Ryan and I went back to Phillip's apartment. The first few days were tough because I was a new, young mother and I didn't know what I was doing. Phillip had sickle cell anemia and was often sick. He was in the hospital when I came home and I was left alone to take care of my baby. David came over every day to see Ryan but that wasn't enough. I needed full time help and we also needed a bigger space because Phillip's apartment was not fit for all of us. I told David my concerns and he began to come around more. We started to do things as a family and eventually we got back together. David was living with his cousin at 16th Street and Girard Avenue. His cousin said it would be okay for me and Ryan to live with them, so I packed up our things and we moved.

When we moved in I was excited because the apartment was much bigger than ours and we had our own room. Tina, David's cousin, was very kind and I appreciated her for allowing us to stay there. She had a son and another roommate, but her three bedroom apartment was big enough for all of us; at least for the moment.

Some time had passed and I had not seen my family since moving in with David. Looking back I am unsure of the reason why but I needed my family. I felt alone and things with David quickly went from stable to rocky. I found out David had been sleeping with the neighbor on the second floor. I suspected there was something going on with the two of them because she often rolled her eyes at me, and she never said hello when I spoke.

Tina felt bad that David was sleeping around on me, especially with someone in the same building, so she confirmed my suspensions. I knocked on the woman's door and confronted her. She wasted no time getting smart with me and that was all I needed to punch her in the mouth. I beat her down and I was fuming. How could David sleep with someone in the same apartment as me and his son? Not that I wanted him cheating on me at all but he had no tack.

Once David got home he ensured me that he did not sleep with her while we were together. His claim was that he had been with her when we were broken up, but that he had ended things with her. I believed him. I didn't want to believe that he could be bold enough to sleep with the neighbor while we were living together. I was so naïve.

A few days later we moved because I could not stay there anymore. I didn't want to see her face and the anger I felt inside would have resulted in me hitting her again. We moved in with David's father, who lived in Mount Airy. At this time I was a junior in high school and my grades were not good. I could not focus because I couldn't find someone consistent to watch Ryan while I went to school. David couldn't do it because he had to work, so my grades suffered.

In my senior year I transferred to Martin Luther King High School because they had a daycare center for teen students. The school was also closer to my house. I reconnected with a former friend named Nashay, who had attended Girls High with me and now lived two doors down from us. It all seemed to be working out.

Walking into King for the first time gave me a culture shock. For three years I had went to a school with all girls. To walk into a school with boys was just unbelievable. With all this testosterone in the building I had to pay more attention to the way I dressed and how my hair was styled. I liked the coed school but it was still new to me.

The second week of school I met another friend named Valerie. She had a daughter that was one year older than Ryan, and she too lived on my street. Instantly we got close. We walked to school every day and we hung out at each other's houses. She worked at McDonald's inside of The Children's Hospital, and I babysat her daughter while she was at her job. We became extremely close and did everything together.

I prospered in King. The classwork was easy and I got along with my teachers. I didn't make too many friends but I was fine with that. Towards the end of the school year Valerie began to hang out with a group of girls and she started to act differently towards me. She didn't want to hang out anymore and we stopped being friends. During the last week of school I was standing in the hallway with my friend, Shontaya, talking; we had just started hanging out. I knew her from Girls High and I used to see her in the neighborhood when we were younger. Valerie walked passed us and Ryan yelled her name out. She ignored him and I cursed her out. I was so upset because she had changed for no apparent reason and walked around with her nose stuck up in the air. After that day I did not speak to her and it would be years later before I saw her again.

By the end of my twelfth grade year, David and I had our own apartment. We stayed in the Olney section of the city and not too long after moving there, I ran into a paternal cousin of mine. Tamika was a police officer and she would visit Ryan and I on her lunch breaks. She gave me my father's contact information. It had been more than eight years but now I was finally able to hear his voice again.

He was now living in Tennessee. I asked him if he could visit us but he said, "I can't come to Philly right now but when I can I will." He never told me the reason why he couldn't come to the city, but I assumed he had done something wrong, and someone may have been looking for him. We talked every day and he sent me money for my graduation. I sent him letters and pictures of Ryan and me. He had to get his neighbor to read the letters I sent because my father could not read. I loved being back in contact with my father. He made me feel safe and like everything was going to be okay. He also believed in me and made me feel like I could do anything that I put my mind to.

During this time my mother was still actively abusing drugs and I didn't have much contact with her. Therefore having a relationship with one of my parents was a true blessing. After several months of being in contact with my father his telephone was disconnected. I knew that he worked at a college as a janitor and that he was not making much money. So I understood the reason his phone could have been turned off. I continued to send him letters but they were returned to me. I assumed he moved but I had nothing concrete to support my theory. This short time that my father returned into my life would be the last time my dad and I spoke; despite my constant efforts to find him.

David was working for a bus company that transported senior citizens to and from their appointments. Our relationship took a dive because he did not help me with Ryan as much as I needed and wanted him to. Don't get me wrong, he was a good provider but I needed more than that. He bought clothes and paid our bills, but he was not hands on with Ryan.

The day that I graduated from high school I wanted to go to a cookout with my friends. I asked David to keep Ryan and he said, "No. Take him with you." I was upset. I always had my son with me and I just wanted to celebrate my graduation. David always went out with his friends and I never had that option. I always had to watch our son. Things just got worse for us. I was eighteen and he was twenty-two. We were playing house and were too young for the responsibilities of a relationship and parenthood.

In June I graduated. In August I was gone. I just couldn't deal with David anymore. Ryan was only two years old.

Chapter 3
Increase

I moved in with my mom on 32nd and Diamond Streets. I was so happy to be back in her presence. When I was around her I always felt happy. At the time I wasn't working so the only contribution I could give was towards food. I was receiving public assistance and I got food stamps. My mom suggested that I take this opportunity to either go back to school or to get a job while I was living with her. I did just that. I found a job in Center City at a familiar department store- Strawbridge and Clothier. Ryan attended a home daycare down the street from the house. For the first time in my life I had a taste of freedom and some independence. I could provide for my son and take a moment for myself when I needed one.

While working at Strawbridge's I became friends with an employee named Sara. We both weren't making much money at the store because we were part time employees. The little pay we got went straight to our children's care and needs. One day while on my lunch break I was shopping for Ryan in Sara's department. She worked in the children's section and she said she would ring me up. However, Sara did not ring up all the items I purchased and we were both terminated for stealing. It was embarrassing and upsetting. I knew no good could come from stealing and it was a lesson I only needed to learn once. I've never did anything like that again.

I was back to square one; unemployed, a single mother, and collecting welfare benefits. When the spring of 1998 arrived, Ryan was two-and-a-half years old. I was still living with my mom on 32nd street but I was not working or in school. I had no direction and I didn't know what I wanted to do with my life. I thought about going to the Community College of Philadelphia but I did not know what steps to take, so I gave up on that idea.

On the weekends I began to hang out with my friends, but other than that nothing was really happening for me. I didn't have much of a life. While most of my friends were working, I was at home with Ryan. With no job, he had to leave the daycare. So I spent the days teaching him his alphabets, numbers, and colors. I could not afford to take Ryan on trips, to museums, or to any of the kid venues, so I took him on walks around the neighborhood. I tried to make the best out of my situation and he always seemed to have a smile on his young face.

On a day in June, while walking Amber and Ryan to the store to get a water-ice, a Black 929 car pulled up beside us. I ignored the honking horn and kept walking. As we began to walk faster a heavyset, tall, and brown skinned guy in a baseball uniform got out of his car and started to walk towards us. I stopped to see what he wanted.

He had a beautiful smile and he said to me, "Hi. What's your name? You're beautiful. How old are you?" I appreciated his compliments and thought it was funny that he had asked a question, gave a compliment, and then asked a question again without getting any responses from me. I asked him for his name and I wanted to know how old he was. "I'm Duke and I'm twenty-six." His age didn't bother me even though I was only nineteen.

We talked for a brief time before he wrote his number down on a dollar bill. I was not amused at all. I was a little irritated because I thought he was showing off. I took his number but I did not want to call him. I had gone on a few dates with other guys, and things didn't work out. I figured going out with him would only produce the same results.

Three days had passed and I still did not call Duke, and I had no intention on phoning him. While standing in the doorway of my house a car pulled up. I did not recognize the man in the car because of my bad vision, and I was not wearing my glasses. The driver of the car was staring at me but I still could not make out his face. After several minutes of staring, the driver parked his car a few doors down from my house. It was Duke and he had a little boy with him.

He approached me and introduced me to his son William. He told me how disappointed he was that I didn't call because he was interested in getting to know me. I listened but I didn't say much. He eventually convinced me to call him. Duke and I talked on the phone several times before we went out on a date. He told me that he owned and operated a barbershop in West Philly and that he was also employed as a drug dealer. Being young and dumb his type of employment didn't bother me at all.

He was so easy to talk to. We talked about everything. I shared details of my childhood with him and he did the same. We had a lot in common and he made me feel like I mattered. After eating dinner on our first date, Duke took me to a hotel. He thought we were going to have sex but I was not having that. Instead we danced and talked all night. Before we fell asleep he said, "Yo, I respect you for not giving me none. Most women have sex with me real quick because they know I have money." Although I was struggling financially and any extra money would have helped me to take care of Ryan, I refused to sell myself short by having sex with him.

On our second date, I had Ryan and my goddaughter Chloe with me. We took the kids to the Dave and Busters restaurant and we had a ball. He connected with the kids immediately. He loved children and it showed during his interaction with them. He thought Ryan was the cutest little boy and I liked the attention he showed my son.

Duke and I had a lot of fun together. He picked me up every day and he took me everywhere he went. He took me shopping to buy clothes for Ryan and me, and he was there for me not only financially but emotionally. When we finally had sex we were in love.

After living with my mom for several months, I decided I wanted to reconnect with my sister. I moved in with Toya, who was now living in the Bartram Village projects. I was excited about living with Toya because over the years we were not as close as we could have been. It felt good to be with my big sister.

Because she lived in public housing her rent was dirt cheap. It may have not been more than fifty dollars. It was agreed that I would use my food stamps to purchase food monthly, and what little cash assistance I got I could pay for half of the rent with no problem.

When I first moved in with Toya everything was fun and easy going. We would sit on the steps with the neighbors all night, laughing and joking. We drank on the weekends and we also had cookouts. We had a ball. But things began to change between Toya and I.

That July she gave me a birthday party for my twentieth birthday. We had a big cookout at the apartment and all of my friends and family attended. Duke bought me a pair of Versace glasses and a tennis bracelet, with the matching chain. This was the second time in my life that I felt special on my birthday. The first time was when Toya gave me a small party when we were still living with our biological mother. Before then I had never had a party.

Later that evening Duke and I went out to dinner. Although I was happy to celebrate my birthday I began to regret moving in with my sister. She began to be very mean to me, despite all my efforts to build and strengthen our bond. I picked up my nieces- Toya now had three children- from school when she had to work. I cooked dinner every night and I made sure the house stayed cleaned. I wasn't working and did all I could to make things easier on Toya; however nothing I did seemed to make her happy with me.

I was scared to come out of my room because I never knew how her attitude would be. Sometimes she talked to me and other times she did not. Sometimes I would hear her talking about me on the phone with her friends. I did not understand why. All I wanted was a relationship with my sister. Finally, I began to confide in Duke about how Toya was treating me and immediately he got me an efficiency apartment in West Philly.

Soon after moving into my apartment I found out I was again pregnant. I was so disappointed with myself but what could I expect? I was having unprotected sex and this was the only realistic outcome. As soon as I found out I was pregnant, I also found out that I was not the only woman Duke was seeing. Again, what did I expect? I was dealing with a young drug dealer that had women throwing themselves at him. I was upset but I did not end things with him.

One day Duke picked me up and told me he wanted to introduce me to his mother. We pulled up on her street and she was sitting outside with a few other women. I was nervous but I got out of the car and he introduced me. I was excited but feeling shy. She seemed very annoyed with my presence. She smiled and bluntly said, "Hello. Be careful messing with Duke." I had no idea what that meant. "Okay," I said, as I quickly got back into the car. The introduction did not go as I had imagined and this was the only mother I had met besides David's. Duke's barbershop was on Lancaster Avenue, which wasn't too far from his mom's, so after the awkward meeting with her we headed there. When we pulled up two little girls were playing outside of the barbershop. Duke told me that one of the girls was his sister, whose name was Deon. I sat in the car while he went in the barbershop and Deon ran up to the window and asked, "Are you Duke's girlfriend?" I smiled and said "Yes," as I waited her reply. "My brother has two girlfriends. Her name is Marcy and then he has you," she said, and then she went back to playing.

I couldn't understand how he had time to have another girlfriend. He stayed with me often and we did everything together. When he got back into the car I asked him if he had a girlfriend and he looked at me and said, "Yes, but I'm leaving her soon." I never asked anything else about her because I believed him. To be honest I didn't care. He did everything for me. He loved me and he took care of me and Ryan. I couldn't ask for anything more.

After the realization that Duke had other women in his life, I still had to deal with the fact that I was pregnant. Duke and I decided that I was too young and unstable to have any more children, so we made the decision that I would get an abortion. I made the appointment at the abortion clinic, located at 38th Street and Lancaster Avenue. The day that I was scheduled to get the procedure I began to have mixed emotions. I wanted my baby. I did not want to have an abortion.

When Duke and I walked into the clinic I told him how I was feeling, and he assured me that everything was going to be okay. I wasn't convinced. He called his mother on the phone and she tried to convince me that the best decision was for me to get the abortion. I wasn't listening to her. She hadn't even wanted to speak to me before but now she wanted to give me advice.

Duke left me in the clinic because he had to run some errands. The nurse called my name and I went into the room. A Lionel Richie song was playing. I can't remember what song it was but it was pretty. When the nurse walked out of the room my mind began to race. I could not have an abortion. I didn't want to. By the time she walked back into the room I was already gone.

I walked to the nearest payphone and I called Toya. I told her what had happened and she said if I wanted to have my baby then I should. The next phone call I made was to Duke. I told him that I had left the clinic. He didn't get upset. He said we would talk about it later.

Later that night Duke barged into my apartment asking me if I was the Feds. He told me that the Federal police were looking for him. They went to his girlfriend's Marcy house, as well as his mother's home searching for him. I was disappointed that he thought I had anything to do with the police, but he didn't know who he could trust- and I was not off limits to his suspensions. I assured him that I was not working with the authorities. That night he stayed with me and we talked about my pregnancy, and how deep in the drug-game he really was. We also talked about money. He had money in my apartment and told me that if anything happened to him I was to give that money to his friend, Marvin. I thought that was odd because Justin was one of his best friends, but I didn't say anything about how I felt.

Duke tried to prepare me for his absence. He knew that going to prison was in his near future. He had tried to introduce me to his family but it was clear that I wouldn't have their support when he got locked up. To them I wasn't his main girlfriend so they dismissed me. One family member was kind to me though, and that was

Duke's paternal grandmother.

Grandma Oray embraced me with loving arms. She told me that Ryan reminded her of her son, Wallace, who went missing in the nineties. He was into some illegal activities and to this day he's never been seen again; dead or alive. She also said she didn't like Duke's girlfriend. We told her that I was pregnant and she assured both Duke and I, that she would be there for me and the kids. She made me feel really good because I didn't communicate with anyone else in Duke's family.

In preparation for his probable departure, I started to look for a job. Duke paid my rent and utility bills, and there was no way I could afford my apartment on the three-hundred-and-sixteen dollars that I received monthly from welfare.

September 24, 1998, was my first prenatal appointment. The night before Duke stayed with me so he could take me to my early morning appointment. He was in between my house and hotels, because he could no longer stay with Marcy. The police had been there several times looking for him. Duke left the apartment in order to warm-up his car. When Ryan and I got to the car, he had a flat tire. I didn't want to miss the appointment so he gave me some money to catch the bus. While saying our goodbyes his phone rang and he told the person on the other line that he was on his way. We kissed and I told him that I would call him after the appointment.

My appointment went well and I found out that my expected due date was April 8, 1999. I was excited about my pregnancy although it was a strong possibility that I was going to be a single mother again. I was so excited to tell Duke about my appointment that when I got in the house I didn't even take my jacket off before calling. He didn't answer. I called several times and he didn't answer. This was not like him. He always answered my phone calls. I kept calling and leaving messages, but he didn't answer the phone.

Finally my phone rang, I was sure it was Duke. When I answered the phone, instead of hearing Duke's voice, I heard the voice of an unfamiliar woman. I asked her who she was and she said, "I'm Marcy." I could not believe it. What did she want and why was she calling me? She asked, "Did you hear from Duke?" I told her no and then she began to tell me all this ridiculous stuff that Duke had allegedly said about me. She went on to say that he called me a dumb young girl, and all he wanted from me was sex.

"Oh really," I said. "I'm sure he would tell you that. You're supposed to be his girlfriend and you're okay with that," I continued. "I'm not okay with anything but you don't matter," she said. "Don't fool yourself. He's not doing all this stuff for me because he wants sex. He's paying my bills, taking care of my son and me. It's much more than that. I'm having his child," I screamed at her. She was pissed and responded, "A baby ain't going to keep him." After I finished telling her how her words meant nothing to me, I hung up on her.

The things she said did not upset me because I knew how Duke felt about me. What I couldn't believe was the guts she had to call me; and to think she called me a dumb young girl. She was the one that needed to grow up.

Shortly after that disturbing phone call my phone rang again. I thought it was Duke but again it wasn't. This time I had the pleasure of speaking with his mother. I was annoyed with her because she was not pleasant to me when I had met her a few weeks earlier.
She told me that I should get an abortion because Duke could be facing a lot of time in prison. At that moment I knew that the Feds had captured Duke and my life would be changed forever. She said, "A baby never kept any man so you should just get rid of it." To add insult to injury,

Marcy chimed in as well. "Wow," is all I could say because I could not believe his mother would call me on three-way call.

I hung the phone up and cried my eyes out. Why would someone's mother suggest I kill my baby? Did she have no emotions in her body at all? I felt so alone and I didn't know when I was going to see Duke again. We had fallen in love in just a short period of time, and he took really good care of me. I felt protected when I was with him and now he was gone.

While crying there was a knock at the door. "Who in the world could this be," I thought to myself. Suddenly I got scared and thought it was the Feds. There were some drugs hidden in socks in my closet and now I thought I was about to be arrested. I slowly walked to the door and opened it. It was Justin. I had only met him one time before, even though he had an apartment in my building. He informed me that Duke was arrested and he was facing a lot of time. Then he asked, "Did Duke leave any stuff here?" I knew he was talking about money and drugs. "No," I said, because Duke told me to give everything he had to Marvin.

Justin was fidgety because he was scared. He frightened me when he said that the Feds were still kicking people doors down looking for Duke's drugs and money. I still didn't tell him anything. I was eager for him to leave so I could get out of there. After again telling him that there was nothing in the apartment, he left. As soon as he left I called Toya and told her what had happened. I needed to come over to her house because I was afraid to stay in the apartment.

I walked thirty minutes to Toya's apartment, at eleven at night. When I got to Toya's I told her what had happened; but it was as if she did not care at all. I felt alone again. I called Marvin and told him where Duke's drugs were in the apartment. He came and got the keys and removed the drugs. When Marvin returned with my keys he told me that they suspected Justin was the one that told on Duke, and how he believed he had set him up earlier that morning.

With Duke in jail, my life began to get very difficult again. I started working as a cashier for Salad Works restaurant. I was only making minimum wage and I tried my best to save my apartment. I wanted to talk with someone about my pains and how I was feeling, but my support system was limited. Grandma Oray and I began to get very close. She was the only person in his family I could contact to find out about Duke. I did meet his brother Tray on many occasions, but since he had a relationship with Marcy, our relationship disappeared.

It became a hard reality but I was going to be raising two children on my own, with no support. Despite all of my hard work I lost my apartment because I could not afford the rent. I had to move back in with Toya. I was determined to get my own place and a better job as soon as I had my baby. When I moved back with Toya she was a bit more supportive, but it was difficult living with her because I did not know what side of the bed she was going to wake up on. On one hand she would have my back, but in an instant her mood could change and I'd have to feel her wrath.

Despite the things we went through, she gave me a baby shower for my baby boy. All of my friends and family attended, and Grandma Oray attended; as well as Duke's sister, Kendra. Kendra and I began talking on the phone. She expressed to me that she knew Duke had serious feelings for me. She said she would make sure she did all she could for her nephew.

Ryir was born on his due date, April 8, 1999. I delivered him at the University of Pennsylvania Hospital. The only people in the hospital room with me during his delivery were the doctors and the nurses. It was then that it hit me. For the next six to ten years I would be raising Duke's baby alone. I didn't cry and I didn't get upset because those where the cards I was dealt. With the strength of God I was going to persevere.

I took Ryir home and Toya had the room set up for us. It only took seven months before things got so bad between she and I that I had to move out. She talked about me to her friends, locked me out of her apartment, and I couldn't use her telephone. The last straw was when Toya told her best friend that she wanted me to move out before the winter arrived. I called her on the phone and asked, "Toya, if you didn't want me in your house why didn't you just ask me to leave?" Toya said that she hadn't said that. Although I was scared of my sister I was tired of her unnecessary mistreatment. I told her that I could no longer give her half my welfare check because I needed to save my money to move out. My feelings were extremely hurt but I had to go. I had two children to take care of and we needed a comfortable place to live.

I began to pray and I asked God for the strength to get a job and apartment. I just wanted to provide for my children. The next day I called my case worker from the welfare office and I asked her to place me in a job placement program. The program was called Welfare to Work. It helped by providing welfare recipients the skills they needed to find jobs, which allowed them to become self-sufficient. The program would assist with childcare; resume building, job searches, and gave monetary incentives to those that found employment.

When I talked to the case worker she was hesitant for me to attend because Ryir was not yet a year old, and that was one of the requirements. However, after telling her my situation she quickly enrolled me in the program. I had two weeks to find child care for the children. In the meantime, Toya's paternal Aunt Brenda, who lived around the corner from her, watched my boys until I found childcare.

On the first day I met with my career development worker, Shana. She explained the program details to me, and the next day she was sending me out in the field to apply for some jobs. During this process I was already looking for an apartment and I found a one bedroom in West Philly. The rent was three-hundred-and-fifty dollars a month. I trusted that I was going to find a job, so I told the owner that I would be able to move in. I needed to wait a few weeks because I needed more money. I had some money saved but I was thirty dollars short on the move-in money. I called Duke's sister Kendra and without hesitation she brought me the money. She also brought me a ton of household items as well. By this time our relationship had grown.

The day after Thanksgiving I went out looking for jobs in Center City. I went into the GAP Outlet store, located at 16th and Chestnut Streets and I asked to speak with a manager. They were hiring and the manager told me to come back the next day for an interview with the store manager. I was so excited because this was the first store I walked into and I had gotten an interview. The very next day I had my interview and was hired on the spot. That's when I called the landlord and took him the security deposit.

When I walked out of my apartment, after signing my lease, I saw a man walking down the street. He stopped me and said his name was Steve, and that he was my neighbor. I told him I was trying to move in but was limited on cash, so I was unsure of how I would get my things in the apartment. Steve said he knew someone with a truck and they would move me for free. I didn't believe him...but what did I have to lose?

Hesitantly, I walked with him around the corner to the man with the truck. Steve had a brief conversation with him, and then I got into the truck with the moving man. During the entire ride I prayed for God's protection because I did not know this man. When I got back to Toya's I called her because she had to pick up my nieces from school. I told her I was moving out and hung up the phone. Then I loaded up the truck with what little items I had. After I got my stuff into my new place, I thanked God for all of his blessings. It felt as if things were just being handed to me. That night, when I went and got the boys, I remember feeling so blessed. We had our own. It was one of the best feelings I had had in my twenty-one years of life.

Within one month I was able to put my children in daycare- thanks to my new job- and we had a place of our own to live in. God is so good! I gave him all the credit for the things that were happening to and for me.

Chapter 4
New Season

My apartment was located on the second floor of what looked like a very old house. To enter into my place you had to climb fifteen squeaky, wooden stairs. If you didn't wear shoes, your feet would surely be filled with splinters from the old, but still effective steps. Though old in appearance and filled with squeaky stairs; my apartment was my paradise.

I converted the living room into my boys' bedroom. The walls in all the rooms had been painted with this gloomy tan color, but I spruced up the boy's room. I placed sports decal all over the walls, got them some bright and colorful curtains, along with a bunk bed and plenty of toys to keep them satisfied. I was a poor single mother but I knew my priorities, and I wanted my children to be comfortable-despite my low income status.

The bathroom and kitchen was just like the rest of the apartment, small and outdated, but I succeeded in making my apartment feel like a home. Each night the children and I ate dinner as a family, and we prayed together. It made my heart melt to see them happy and I wanted to give them all I could. I was twenty-one, single, raising two children, and working a minimum wage job.

Life was tough but I was making what I had work for me and my boys.

While employed at the GAP I moved up quickly. When I first started I was a seasonal employee. I did so well after the holiday season that I was promoted to a full time position. After working for the company less than a year, I was promoted to head cashier. I made several friends while working there. One of my closest friends was a woman named Cynthia. Cynthia and I shared similar interests and we clicked. All of my childhood friends lived in Mount Airy and I did not get to see them often, so I was pleased to have met Cynthia.

We both were single parents and we didn't live that far from one another. On the weekends when Ryan was with his dad and Ryir with his grandmother-Duke's mother- Cynthia and I went to the clubs and house parties. Duke's mother and I had finally set aside our differences. She was an excellent grandmother to my son and had become very supportive of me. I had a lot of fun hanging out with Cynthia. She knew how to have a good time.

Some weekends when I had the kids with me, I would take them out during the day and then drop them off to my biological mother's house at night. Although she was still abusing drugs, she wanted to be a part of the boy's life; and I allowed her to do that. During this time I had gone out with several guys but nothing was serious. I wanted to party and if there was one, Cynthia and I were there. I was young and I wanted to enjoy my life.

In 2001 after filing my first income tax, I furnished my apartment and purchased my first car. I bought a 1997 yellow, Mitsubishi Mirage. I loved my car! I was so proud of myself. I was doing well at my job and I was finished with the Welfare to Work program. Financially, I was now about to take care of my children and myself.

Although everything was going okay, I must

admit that I was lonely. I really wanted to be in a serious relationship and to settle down. I was an independent woman but I was tired of doing everything on my own. If I had to struggle I wanted to do it as a family, but finding the right person was tough. Every time I thought I found someone that I could be in a committed relationship with it never worked out. I wanted to be loved. I wanted someone to make me feel the way Duke had made me feel...but I continued to come up empty-handed. So I continued to go to parties with Cynthia and gave up on finding anyone I could take seriously.

On Labor Day weekend in 2001, I had just dropped the kids off on a Saturday afternoon to my mother's house. I had taken them out earlier in the day and now I wanted a little free time. I was driving home as I blasted my favorite song, "Adore" by Prince on my car stereo. I was having a good day so far and I wanted to go home to take a nap before going out with Cynthia.

On that hot summer day I was wearing a pair of sky blue mini shorts, a fitted tee shirt, and flip flops. I was looking good and I knew it. When I arrived home, I parked the car across the street from my apartment because there weren't any parking spots in front of my door. When I got out of the car my neighbor Steve, and another guy, were sitting on his steps. The guy sitting with Steve was very nice looking. He was about 5'7; light skinned, and had a head full of curly hair. His lips were very thin, but they looked sexy and his goatee was trimmed perfectly. I liked the way he looked and it was obvious that he was digging me because he wouldn't stop staring.

"Hello," I said to Steve and the mystery guy, as Steve and his friend walked over to me. When they got to my steps he smiled and said, "Hi, my name is Clarence. Steve is my Uncle." With those few words he spoke I felt an instant connection to him. Steve walked away and Clarence and I sat on my steps. We talked for hours as we drank Coronas and Coolers. I told him about my boys and my life, and he shared a few details of his life with me. He told me that he had one son but that he was not his biological child. He said the boy's real father was not in his life, and since he had a connection with the boy he stayed in his life after he ended the relationship with his mother. I respected him for that.

We talked about our jobs; Clarence said he was a skycap at the airport. He was the youngest child and the only son his mother had. He had a sister but they were not close; yet he was crazy about his niece. His mother was a single mom and his father was absent from his life. His dad had died a few years earlier from a heart attack. I shared with him how I was taken away from my biological mother and raised by my aunt. I told him how I was searching for my father but had no leads. As well as how I longed to talk to my father again. Clarence was very understanding and a good listener. I liked Clarence. He had a rough childhood just like me, and his mother was also addicted to drugs when he was a child. There were a lot of similarities in our childhood.

Clarence was thirty-one and at the time I was only twenty-three, but I didn't let that stop my attraction towards him. I liked him. It also didn't bother me when he told me that he had a girlfriend, because if I can be honest I was used to being second. He did say that he was tired of her and that he was leaving her; and just like before when Duke had spoken those words, I believed him as well. After a long evening of talking, we exchanged numbers and he left when his male friend came to pick him up.

The following day Clarence was on my mind all day. I picked the kids up from my mother's house and went about my regular week, as I waited for Clarence's call. A few days later I saw Clarence inside the newsstand next to my duplex. "What are you doing," I asked, as I saw him standing inside. "I rented this stand out so I can make a few extra dollars," he said. I had no reason to believe that it was all a front for him to sell his drugs out of. That day was the first time he saw Ryan and Ryir, and they seemed to like him. My children meant everything to me so it was very important for them to like him and vice versa. Clarence and I became very close, very fast. I viewed him as my knight in shining armor...but soon I would see a side of him that would have me questioning his true intent.

Ryan's father cut his hair on the weekends when he stayed with him, so I had to find a barbershop for Ryir. Around the corner from my apartment there was a barber named Mike who was good with my son. He made him feel comfortable in the chair and knowing his father was in jail, he rarely charged me to cut my son's hair. As the relationship with my son and Mike grew, he sometimes offered to take Ryir to different events in the city. One evening after I got home from work, I agreed that Mike could take Ryir to a basketball game. Clarence was outside when I was about to take Ryir around the corner, but he didn't speak to me. He seemed highly upset. I asked his uncle what was wrong and he said that Clarence was mad at me for allowing Mike to take Ryir to the game.

I walked over to Clarence and we started to talk. He thought I was dating Mike. I explained to him that I wasn't seeing Mike and that he was simply fond of Ryir. "It don't matter how fond he is of Ryir! I don't want him taking him nowhere. I'll take him to the games and anywhere else he needs to go. His dad's not around and I'll be the missing link, but Mike can't take him nowhere!"

That night not only did Ryir not attend the basketball game but Mike never cut his hair again.

Chapter 5
Trials

September 11, 2001, was a terrible time in America. I was still working at the GAP in center city when we were attacked by terrorist. When the news broke the city was in an uproar. Ryan's school called me and said all children needed to get picked up immediately. Ryir was at his daycare in West Philly and I was scared to death. I didn't know if we were safe or if the attacks would end. I remember calling Clarence and he was very concerned about us. He wanted to make sure we were okay and said he didn't know what he'd do if anything happened to us. He poured out his emotions to me over the phone and even with my worries, I began to feel safe. It felt very good to be cared for so deeply by someone. I had not felt that way in a long time. Clarence was considerate, charming, respectful, and he loved my boys. I had fallen in love with him and I wanted to spend my life with him.

We began to go out often. We took trips to Atlantic City, to New York, and we went to dinner at various restaurants. We also took the kids out and did the many things they wanted to do. He was turning into my everything and I had hoped he was feeling the same way about me. I knew things were progressing quickly but I didn't see a reason to put a timetable on our love.

Our connection was on a high but the relationship between me and my landlord had gone sour. When I first met Clarence I was one month behind on my rent. I went to court to get the issue resolved. The judge created a payment-plan that would allow me to get caught up on my rental payments. The day I was supposed to pay the rent, I didn't end up paying because Clarence was upset. The neighbors had reported to my landlord that he was selling drugs out of my home. My landlord wanted nothing more to do with me and he didn't want Clarence in his building. He said he would get the cops involved and when I told Clarence he moved us. His female friend had a duplex around the corner from us and that is where we moved.

By this time Clarence had indeed left his girlfriend. So we were officially together and moved in as a family. As quickly as things started to look up, things began to change. Clarence became very possessive and was concerned about the clothes I wore. I have always had a small frame. Even with two children I weighed 120 pounds and wore a size two. Clarence wanted to know why I wore tight fitting clothes. I didn't understand him. It was not that I was wearing revealing or tight clothes, I tried to explain to him I only wore clothes that fit my slender body.

He did not like my response. He did not want any other man looking at me and we went shopping so I could get new clothing. Everything he bought was a size eight. I was slipping out of the clothes but since I loved him and didn't want to argue, I agreed to wear the oversized clothing. He was very pleased with my decision and said that he loved me...but he was not done. He didn't want me talking to my friends on the phone anymore, or going out with them for that matter. He said all we needed was each other and the children. I was very foolish. I thought he was showing his true love and concern for me, so I agreed to these conditions as well.

He wanted to know everything about me and he started asking me about Duke. I felt strange divulging any information about him, so I told him things had been good with us and that he had gotten locked up for selling drugs. Clarence told me that he knew Duke. He said that he knew people who knew Duke, and that they wanted to kill not only him, but our son Ryir and me also. He told me that pictures were being taken of us because hit men were crafting a plan to kill us. The only reason why they didn't kill us was because of their loyalty to Clarence.

I was shaken. To think someone wanted to kill my son and I, for no good reason, was simply unbearable. We hadn't done anything to anyone and I couldn't have that happen. Clarence was my protection and he really cared about me and the boys. So what he asked of me, I did. I could not have been dumber.

My continued employment with the GAP began to become questionable. After being a model employee for two years I started to arrive late often, and I called out a lot. Clarence wanted me with him all the time and whenever he demanded that I call out, I did. After being reprimanded by my supervisor about my unacceptable actions, I decided to get my act together. I loved my job and I didn't want to lose it. I had struggled to get me and my boys in a place of our own, and to provide for them so I knew what I had to do.

One morning after taking the kids to school and daycare, I came back home to get dressed for work. Clarence asked me to stay home and I said, "I can't do that baby. I have to go to work, on time, or they'll fire me." He continued to pester me about staying home but I kept getting dressed. When I proceeded to leave out of the apartment, Clarence pushed me. I fell down a flight of steps. When I hit the floor it felt like I had been knocked out by a heavyweight boxing champion. I got up off the floor and ran out of the apartment, straight down Market Street. I did not know where I was going but I had to get away from him. I was scared. I was delirious and unsure of what had just happened.

While I was running Clarence pulled alongside of me in his car and said, "It was an accident. I swear I would never do anything to hurt you. You know I love you and the boys. You're all I have. Don't run away. Baby, this is just a misunderstanding. Let me make it right." I believed him. There was no way that he would have pushed me down a flight of stairs. Clarence loved me and he would never hurt me. Those were the thoughts that raced through my mind as we drove back to the house. When I got upstairs I called out of work because I was in too much pain to come in. This was the beginning of the physical abuse.

Clarence was extremely jealous and controlling. He began to believe that I was sleeping with every man I came in contact with. Whether it was a stranger crossing the street, or a driver that might be in my view while we stopped at a stop sign or a red light; according to Clarence I was sleeping with all of them. Nothing I did or said convinced him otherwise.

The caring and loving Clarence that I had grown to love began to fade daily. He became very demanding and difficult to be around. I grew to fear him. I could not look at another man, and while that was almost impossible, he came up with a plan that worked for him but it caused me great pain.

While driving to the mall with Clarence, who was sitting in the passenger seat, I pulled up to a stop sign. A man who was crossing the street walked across, and when the street was clear I pulled off. Without warning Clarence punched me in my ribs. I did not see it coming but I could feel the excruciating pain. He grabbed my mouth and said, "Shut up. Every time I see you look at another man this is what's going to happen to you. Don't sit there and act like you didn't look at him either!"

Through my tears I asked him what was I supposed to do if a man walked in front of the car. He harshly replied, "You better put your damn head down or I'll end up breaking your ribs. And while we at it you better keep your head down when we're walking too. You so busy looking at everyone else when you need to be focusing on me."

Driving with him was torture. While I drove he positioned the passenger side mirror towards my direction. He did this because he wanted to see everything I looked at. When he wasn't looking in the mirror he stared directly in my face. If I stopped at a stop sign or a red light; he eyed me as men walked by. I placed my head down so he could see I was not looking at anyone. But if he thought I looked at a man, which he often did even when I wasn't, he'd punch me in my ribs. I couldn't even walk anywhere with him. If my head wasn't low towards the ground he'd hit me. My life was turning into a living hell.

I couldn't do anything. I was isolated from my friends and family. The rare times I talked to Toya I never shared with her, or anyone else for that matter, the abuse I was going through. I had no one. How was I going to leave the man that helped take care of my children? The man who was protecting Ryir and I from the hit men that wanted us dead? How was I going to leave the man I loved, yet I was grossly afraid of?

When Clarence wasn't being mean and abusive, he would convert back into the man I fell in love with. He was sweet and caring. He proposed to me and I accepted. I accepted out of fear and in that fear I truly thought I loved him.

On the day of my wedding my gut kept telling me

not to marry him, but I did it anyway. On a gloomy day in March of 2002, I married Clarence after only being together for six months. We were married at a wedding salon in Upper Darby, Pennsylvania. Clarence's mother wasn't too pleased with me because she felt he should have married his previous girlfriend. However, despite her feelings towards me she came to the wedding to support her son. My sister Toya had come as well.

During the five minute ceremony my spirit kept telling me not to go through with it but I didn't listen. For some strange reason I believed that if I married Clarence things would change. I thought I could prove to him how much I loved him and how much I wanted him to be a part of our lives.

I was such a silly girl. Nothing changed about Clarence. The evil inside of him only got worse. Clarence began to beat me on a regular basis. I did my best to oblige him and to follow his every rule to escape his punishments, but nothing worked. Often I was beat because he thought I was cheating on him. Even though I never went anywhere but straight to work, to pick up the children, and then back home. I got beaten so much that I cannot remember every incident. It became as normal as taking a breath. Although Clarence treated me terribly and beat me, he never physically hurt the children.

The summer of 2002 slowly approached. By this time I was working at a GAP store in the Gallery Mall. Clarence showed up to my job whenever he felt like it, and he never called first to say he was coming. He would call the job often to ensure I was there, and each time I took my break I was commanded to call him. If he called the store and I was not available because I would be helping a customer, I knew that night I would be in trouble. Our relationship was an exasperating emotional roller coaster. When things were good we'd take the kids on trips and he'd take me out. He treated me like a princess when he was happy with me. When things were bad, they were bad.

Clarence never apologized after he beat me. Instead he'd take me to the mall and buy me expensive gifts or take me out. When things were going well I held on to the hope that the last fight was the last beaten he'd ever give me. But there was always another reason to give me plenty more.

One afternoon I loaded the car with bags of laundry to take to the Laundromat. When I opened the trunk of the car I found a disposable camera. Clarence and I would often take pictures of the kids with disposable cameras, but this camera did not look familiar. I asked Clarence what was on the film and he said, "None of your business and don't get those pictures developed." I took the camera to the one hour photo center. When I finished washing I picked up the pictures. I couldn't believe what was on that roll of film. Clarence and a friend of his named, Jaleel, were naked along with some girl. There were pictures of them having sex and doing all sorts of sexual acts. The pictures were taken inside of his mother's house. I was in disbelief. He was beating me because he thought I was sneaking around when all the while he was cheating on me. "How could he do this to me," I said softly, staring at the photographs. I became sick to my stomach. I was so hurt but my pain quickly turned to anger.

When I got back to the apartment I was crying hysterically. I yelled at him. I wanted answers for what he had done but he was not about to make this about him. He told me it was my fault because I never should have gotten the pictures developed. I yelled louder, "How can you beat me for cheating when that's what you've been out here doing! And you had the nerve to take her to your mom's house!"

I sent Ryir to his room and that day Ryan was

with his dad. I went into the bedroom and started packing our clothes because I was leaving Clarence. Before I could get all of our clothes packed he came into the room. "What are you doing," he asked. "I'm done with this. I'm leaving you," I said, as I took the bag and began to move towards the bedroom door. "You're not going anywhere," he said, as he grabbed me by my neck and threw me across the room. I tried to run away from him but it only made matters worse.

He repeatedly threw me across the room and then he proceeded to beat me with a broom. He had rage in his eyes and I knew he was going to kill me. Every blow was harder than the one before. I screamed and I cried. Ryir ran into the room but I could not let him see this man torture me. I screamed at my son to go back into his bedroom, and with tears falling from his youthful eyes he left.

Clarence was enraged and the appearance of my son did not stop the beaten. He dropped the broom and picked up a bottle of Alize, and then he poured the alcohol all over me. Next he picked up a box fan and started hitting me with it. The fan was too big and he could not control how he hit me with it, so he put it down. Next he began to punch me with all of his might. I begged Clarence to stop but he didn't. I prayed and asked God to stop the beating before I took my last breath, but Clarence kept hitting me.

I tried to fight back but that only made matters worse. The hate in his eyes scared me until I thought I'd rather die than to see that type of evil up close. Something inside of me kept trying to get away from this 200 pound man, but he overpowered me without effort. I was defeated. I lost all of my strength and became very weak. I went in and out of consciousness. When I lost full consciousness he grabbed me by my neck, sat himself on the chair, and dumped my lifeless body on the floor by him.

He then wrapped his legs around me so I could not move, as he propped my head up and begin his next level of torture. Too weak to move, I heard the sound of clippers and he started to shave my head.

A few hours later I had awaken from the brutal beat down. Clarence was sitting on the bed across from me staring at me. He ordered me to get up and get myself together. I went into the bathroom and when I looked in the mirror, it was a horrid sight. I had bald spots all over my head and bruises covered most of my body. Although I was used to wearing my hair short, I knew this would be hard to hide. He had ruined my hair. And I was used to hiding bruises but these would be difficult to cover because they were all over.

When I got myself together I called Ryir's grandmother so he could go over her house for the weekend. I got Ryir's things together and was about to get in the car when Clarence said, "Oh, the city towed your car." This couldn't be happening to me. Not today, and not all in the same day. I had just been beat within inches of my life and the only thing I owned, that got me back and forth to work, and my children to and from daycare and school, had been taken from me. I asked Clarence to take me to Ryir's grandmother's house so I could drop him off and he agreed. Before we left he never directly commented on my hair or the bruises. He simply said, "Put a hat on your head."

When we got outside my car was parked directly in front of our apartment, but all of the windows had been broken out. He threw a brick through all of my windows while I was unconscious. The brick was still sitting on the front seat of the car. The city did not tow my car but Clarence had destroyed it. He also said I shouldn't worry about getting the windows fixed because he had poured sugar in my tank.

When I took Ryir to his grandmother's she asked

if I was okay. I told her that I would be and it was clear she knew I was having some problems in my relationship. The bruises were fresh and they could be seen, and this was not the first time Clarence had tatted me up from his beatings. She knew I was being abused but there was nothing she could do. I also had a feeling she was going to tell Duke how badly I looked this time. There was something in her eyes that said she could no longer lie to him about what was really going on with me.

After we dropped Ryir off, we went to Clarence's mother's house. While I knew she didn't like me, I didn't mind being around because she never did or said anything disrespectful; until this day. Ms. Laura knew that her son was abusing me but she never concerned herself with his doings. Often times she would ask me, "Girl what did you do to rile him up?" She blamed me for her son punching and kicking me.

When we went into her house he told her what had happened and she asked me, "Why did he shave your hair?" Instantly I hated her. She was worried about my hair instead of addressing the real problem. He was abusing me, and it would have been nice if she said something to make him stop, or to go seek treatment, but she was worried about my hair. I began to think that at some point in her life she was abused because she was numb to my pain. She showed no concern and had no empathy.

I began to talk to Toya whenever I could. I told her what Clarence had done to me and she was very upset. She had been in an abusive relationship before so she understood exactly what I was going through. She told me that I could live with her if I wanted to. When I was at work I would stop by her job, which was also downtown, and we would talk. My abusive relationship weighed so heavy on my sister's heart that she began to have anxiety attacks. She wanted to kill Clarence but we both knew that was just a wish.

The emotional roller coaster and cycle of violence was a part of my daily routine. When Clarence was not physically, verbally, and mentally abusive, he was winning and dining me. He continued to take me out to nice restaurants and still bought me expensive gifts. The cycle was very confusing. I thought I was going to lose my mind, and several times I thought suicide was my only way out.

When February 2003 arrived, I had lost a substantial amount of weight. I was barely working and the only joy I received came from my two boys. In that month David had petitioned the courts for full custody over Ryan. I was a good mother and I worked very hard to take care of my children, but the fact that I was being abused was a reality the David would no longer ignore. To be honest, I knew the abuse was causing my parenting skills to diminish. I could not fully be there for the boys because I was always in such horrible shape; physically and mentally. My children had witnessed my sufferings firsthand and David was afraid of the impact it was having on Ryan. He was also afraid that Clarence would abuse Ryan.

When I received the custody papers in the mail I wasn't surprised. David knew what was going on and he wanted his son out of that environment. The thing that was shocking was the beating I received, because Clarence thought I had told David about the abuse when he saw the custody papers. I did not need to tell David because his eyes could see the bruises, and what he did not see Ryan filled in. The hearing was scheduled for March of that same year.

On the morning of the hearing I got into another fight with Clarence. I arrived late and by the time I got there I had lost primary physical custody of my son. I was awarded weekend and summer visitation. I love my sons with all of my heart. I did not want to separate them or to have them living outside of the home, but I knew Ryan was in a safer environment. Although it hurt to the core that I did not have my son fulltime, this was the best living arrangement for him. I had wished Duke was home from prison so he could have taken Ryir to live with him. I didn't want either of my sons to witness their mother being abused.

Realizing that I needed some kind of help, I looked back to a place that had always made me feel whole. I was a member of the Liberty Christian Bible Fellowship Church and so I returned. Surprisingly, Clarence joined me. One Sunday as the preacher did the alter call, requesting that if anyone wanted to give their lives to Christ they should come forward, Clarence stood up. He confessed that he was a sinner and Jesus died on the cross to save his soul.

I praised God because Clarence was now saved. I knew that as a little girl when I was saved it had changed my life. God was always with me even when I had stopped going to church. I knew that God could change things, but somewhere along the way I had stopped believing that he would deliver me from the bondage that I was in. But as Clarence stood at the alter I was renewed in my faith. I knew that Clarence's life would change for the better and the man I fell in love, God would restore him whole and we would live happily ever after.

Clarence attended church with me on a weekly basis and he enjoyed going. I talked to him about going to marriage counseling with the pastor, because despite our attendance at church our marriage was in trouble. He agreed.

During our first counseling session Clarence lied when the pastor asked if there was any abuse in our relationship. He said no, and I didn't have the courage to tell the truth. This was Clarence and I was still walking on eggshells. What I did confess was Clarence's constant accusations of me cheating. The pastor asked, "Clarence is this true," and he responded, "Yes."

I was excited because this was a breakthrough. He told the pastor that he often thought I was cheating. How he had seen a random man on his cellphone and he was sure the man was talking to me on the other end. Sounds crazy but these were the constant thoughts walking around in my husband's head. I thought the pastor would have outright called Clarence nuts but he was calm. He listened as Clarence spoke and when he was finished the pastor responded.

"You know it would be impossible for your wife to be on the phone with all these random guys you see talking on their phones. She loves you and she wants to be with you. It was her choice to marry you and you have to work on yourself in order to build a healthy relationship with your wife, and your family. I want to help you and God will be able to remove these thoughts from your mind and give you peace. Love is not jealous and you can't live your life constantly accusing the woman you love of cheating. Let's work on building a stronger foundation with God and strengthening your marriage."

I was relieved that Clarence was listening with such intent. It was as if he understood exactly what the pastor had said to him, and I was overjoyed. I knew the abuse would end and I could have the marriage I always wanted. Yet, my life with Clarence was as inconsistent as it comes. One moment happy, the next I'm living in a horror film. After just three counseling sessions Clarence did not want to go anymore because he said the pastor wanted to sleep with me. He was back to his crazy way of thinking. Oh, and since he thought the pastor wanted me I wasn't allowed to be around him anymore. We stopped going to church.

I was so upset. Walking to the alter and pledging his love for Christ had gotten us nowhere. He was only doing those things to quiet my mouth for a spell, but he could only contain the true Clarence for a little while. Now he was back to his normal crazy and abusive self. I started to feel sorry for myself. I was trapped, scared, and desperate for a way out...but I didn't feel I had the strength to leave him or the support system. I was afraid that he would kill me and anyone else who got involved with our situation.

During one of the many honeymoon stages of our marriage, Clarence took me to the mall to buy some items for the kids. Things were going great. He was making jokes and I was laughing and feeling upbeat. The fun quickly ended when Clarence accused me of flirting with a guy who was in the store where we were shopping. He said I was following the guy around the store. I did not know who he was talking about. My eyes never made contact with another man when I was out with Clarence, let alone would I be stupid enough to flirt with one. I always made sure I walked with my head down because I did not want my ribs to become Clarence's personal punching bag. His mind was set and I knew there would be consequences for the psychotic thoughts that plagued his mind. Immediately, I didn't want to go home. I knew what would happen.

While driving home he didn't say so much as a word the entire ride. Instead he stared at me as if he was reading my mind and trying to extract my soul. I was filled with fear. In that moment I'd rather die than continually be beat for incidents that only happened inside of Clarence's mind.

When we got home he began to push me around, but he didn't punch or slap me. "You're a whore and I hope you don't think anyone else wants you! You're damaged goods and you got two kids by two different men. Don't nobody want a whore like you," he yelled out to me. I was used to his verbal lashings but the words still hurt. Every chance he got he degraded me and he did it so often that I started to believe every word he said.

I thought that maybe I was off the hook because he was only throwing his words at me, but quickly things escalated. Clarence pushed me on the bed. "You f******g whore," he screamed, as he punched me on the side of my face; right next to my eye. I was crying hysterically. Why was he doing this to me? I could not beat him. I hadn't done anything. I was his wife and I wanted him to feel sorry for me. I wanted him to apologize and stop hitting me. To stop verbally abusing me and to get help, but he wouldn't. He had to hate me but I didn't know why. I did everything he wanted me to do. I was a good wife. I cooked, I cleaned, and I had sex with him whenever he wanted it. I catered to his every need and want, but it was never enough.

After he punched me he told me that my eye would be black in the morning. I jumped up and looked in the mirror but it was not black. It looked fine so I did not believe him. I got myself together because both of my children were home. I knew they had heard everything but I didn't know what to say to them. I cooked dinner, fed them, and then got the kids ready for bed.

The next morning the kids were already in the living room when I got out of the bed. I walked towards them to give them a kiss and hug. Both Ryan and Ryir started screaming as I approached them. I did not know why they were crying until Ryan asked, "Mom what's wrong with your eye?" I ran into the bathroom to see what Ryan was talking about. When I looked in the mirror my entire left eye was black and a portion of my right eye was too. He was right. I told the kids I was okay, although I knew that I wasn't. Then it dawned on me that I had to go in to work. How was I going to go to my job with black eyes? How was I going to go out in public with my face looking the way it did? I decided that I had to stay in the house the entire weekend, because even with sunglasses I had none large enough to cover my black eyes. The bruising stopped at the top of my cheeks so it was very difficult to cover.

Monday morning I asked Clarence if he could take me to take Ryir to school. "No. You ain't going nowhere with you d**n eyes looking like that," he said. That morning he left the house and I did not see him for a few days. I had only been working at this new GAP location for a few months. I had to call my store manager and lie. I told him that I was in a car accident and would need a leave of absence for a couple of weeks. He believed me and told me to take care of myself. He assured me my job would be waiting for me when I got back. Hiding the abuse from my family, friends, and coworkers was a task I did well. I never talked about it and the bruises that I normally received from Clarence were easily covered with my clothing. So if I wanted to keep the abuse under wraps I knew I could not venture out in my current condition.

During Clarence's absence I called my friend Shontaya. I shared with her a few things I was going through, but I minimized most of it. She told me about an agency she had heard about. They assisted abused women and the name of the program was the Lutheran Settlement House. She said maybe they could help me. I took down the number but I was too embarrassed to call. How was I going to tell a stranger that I was allowing another human being to beat me; and to control every aspect of my life?

I started to think about my life and the direction I wanted it to go in. I had lost my self-worth. I didn't know who I was anymore. I had lost custody of my son, I had lost weight, and each day I stayed with Clarence I was closer to losing my life. I tried everything in my power to please him. There was nothing else that I could do. I hated myself. I decided to try to get my life back together and since Clarence was already gone, this was the perfect opportunity for me to do so.

The next morning I woke up very early. I wanted to take Ryir to daycare, and I needed to go to the emergency room because my eyes still had not cleared up. Also, I was going to get a Protection From Abuse (PFA) order. I was finally going to leave Clarence. I know I had said that a hundred times but this morning I was ready to put my plan into action.

While on Septa's el-train I saw a friend of mine named Saheed. Saheed often shopped at my job for his daughter and he had dated Cynthia once. I had lost contact with her because I allowed Clarence to isolate me. Instantly, he noticed my black eyes-despite the sun glasses I was wearing-and asked me if Cynthia had known about the abuse. I knew she had a feeling that I was being abused and I finally came clean to him. I confirmed the rumors. I don't know why I had let out my secret but maybe I was just tired of holding all my pain inside. I told Saheed that I was on my way to get a PFA, then to the hospital, and that I was going to move in with my sister to get away from Clarence. He hugged me and then gave me his number. "When you've got everything packed call me. I'll come get you and help you move your stuff. This is messed up and I don't want to see you like this. Make sure you call me," he said. I put Saheed's number in my pocket and got off the train to handle my business.

My first stop was family court. I needed protection from Clarence and had to get a protection order quickly. Reluctantly, I told the court clerk in detail what had happened to me. I was so embarrassed. I thought the clerk was judging me because I had stayed in the relationship so long. I thought everyone was staring at me because my eyes looked terrible. I took my sunglasses off inside of the building so she could see the bruises, and without further delay I was granted a temporary PFA by the judge.

I was told I had to have someone else serve Clarence a copy. The clerk suggested I use a police officer if I did not have anyone else to do it. She also said we both had to appear in court if I wanted to get a permanent order. The thought of Clarence finding out I was getting a PFA, having it served to him by a police officer, and then sitting across from him in a courtroom to get a permanent order had me soaked in fear. He was currently wanted by the police because he did not go to court for a pending drug charge. He hated the police and he did not want anything to do with them, and now I needed the cops to give him a protection order. It was a hard reality to fathom.

After leaving the court I walked to Thomas Jefferson Hospital. The doctor said my eyes would heal but it would take time. There was nothing they could do for me. I remember thinking why hadn't he asked me what happened to my eyes. I wanted to tell him because I thought in some way he could help me get out of the hell I was living in. But he never asked.

While walking back to the train I kept thinking there was someone coming to recuse me. I wanted someone to understand my pain. On the train ride home I prayed and asked God to let my home be empty. I didn't want Clarence to be home and I was afraid. I had been gone all day and if he was there and I wasn't, it would be a problem. I still was worried about who would serve him the PFA. My fears were constant and gave me uncontrollable anxiety.

When I got to the apartment Clarence's scooter was parked in front of the door. I was shook. I did not know what was going to happen. I slowly opened the door and took my time climbing the steps. I did not want to see him. When I walked in the room he was lying across the bed with his eyes closed. There was a letter next to him. He opened his eyes and asked me to read the letter. I slowly read the two page apology letter. In the letter he said as a child he watched his mother abuse drugs, and that men had abused her. He wrote that he had learned his abusive behavior, but that he did not want to be this way. He promised that he would never hit me again. I believed the things he said about his mother but there was no way I was going to believe that he would never hit me again. I was tired of being tired and I wanted my marriage with Clarence, the life I had shared with him, and the constant abuse to end.

After reading the letter Clarence continued to apologize. I told him that I didn't want to be with him anymore. He continued to promise that he'd never hit me again. He pledged to get help and work hard to be a better man and husband. Nothing he said convinced me but I listened as he cried and pleaded.

"Where were you? What took you so long to get home," Clarence asked, in the middle of his pleading. "I got a restraining order and I went to the emergency room to have my eyes checked out," I said, and now I was afraid that he would punch me in the face again. "You got what," he shouted. I didn't want to repeat myself. "It don't take that long. You was out with some dude," he yelled.

He began to accuse me of being with another man. I begged him to believe me but nothing I said convinced him. He told me to take my clothes off. Up until that moment I forgot that I had Saheed's number in my pants. I kept telling Clarence that I was in court and the hospital. I even showed him the paperwork to prove it, but he didn't care. "Stop talking and take your clothes off," he demanded. I did what he said because I knew if I didn't he would hit me.

When I took my pants off Saheed's number fell out of my pocket. I stopped breathing. This was it. Clarence was going to kill me. I tried to pick up the paper before he saw it but it was too late. He picked the paper up off the floor and read it. "Who is this dude," he yelled. "He's Cynthia's man. He was going to help me move out. I swear that's all. He just wanted to help me because he saw my eyes and he said Cynthia's been worried about me."

I couldn't tell if he believed me or not. He was filled with hate. "Look me in my face b***h! Now tell me the truth," he demanded. I repeated my story, assuring him that every word I spoke was accurate. "Even if that's the case no man should be offering another man's wife no ride. I don't care what's going on," he said. "I understand. It will never happen again," I said. "Good." After that he left it alone.

I picked Ryir up from daycare and cooked dinner. I felt like everything was okay until Clarence began to question me about Saheed again. I kept repeating the same facts but he wouldn't stop questioning me. "So if I ask Saheed what happened, is he going to tell me the same thing," Clarence said. "Of course he is because nothing happened," I said.

Clarence instructed me to get Ryir in the car because we were going to a payphone. I asked him why. What a mistake. He pulled a gun out of his pocket and placed it midway on my back, and said, "You need to do exactly what I tell you or I'm going to kill you." My entire body tensed up as I looked at Ryir. I knew that night my life would end. I put Ryir in the car and we drove down the street to the pay phone. Clarence kept his gun pointed at me and had no consideration for my son, who was in the car scared to death. I could barely breathe but I had to stay calm for Ryir. I knew Clarence was capable of killing me because he had told me stories of how he had shot people in his past. Prior to that night I did not believe that he had shot anyone, but tonight it was clear that he was capable of murder.

When we got to the payphone he told Ryir to stay in the car. It was about nine-thirty at night and although it was the summertime there was no one outside; which was rare for the neighborhoods in West Philly. When we got out of the car he kept his gun pointed to my back. I thought he was going to kill me on the spot. I was thinking of ways to get out of the situation but I could not come up with anything, especially when I looked in the car and saw Ryir's innocent eyes watching our every move.

"Pick up the phone," Clarence said, as he handed me the piece of paper with Saheed's number on it. "Call him," he shouted. "What are you going to do," I asked. "Nothing. I just want to make sure yall stories match. If they do you don't have anything to worry about." I didn't believe. He said, "Don't act scared or sound funny. If you act stupid I'll kill you first and then I'll deal with Ryir. Tell Saheed to meet you at the corner of 59th and Arch Street in fifteen minutes."

I called Saheed and told him that I needed to talk to him. I asked him to meet me at the location Clarence wanted and he said he'd be there in fifteen minutes. He asked if I was really okay, and I lied and said yes. I wanted to say no. I wanted to tell him the truth but I couldn't. I had a gun pointed at me, along with the promise I'd be killed-as well as my son-if I didn't follow my husband's commands. I wanted to die and at this point no one could save me but God.

Once Saheed agreed to meet me I hung the phone up. We got back in the car and Clarence still had his gun pointed at me. When we got back to the apartment he told me to put Ryir in bed. I did what he said and then we walked to 59th and Arch Streets; which was directly around the corner from our apartment. The entire walk there I was petrified and Clarence hadn't put his gun away. I knew he was not about to talk to Saheed. I could feel that something terrible was about to take place. During the walk, Clarence kept reminding me that if I ran, screamed or looked scared, he would shoot me in my back and get rid of my body. Too afraid to make a mistake I followed his every command.

Once we got to Arch Street, he told me to stand on the corner near the telephone booth. He hid on the porch next door to my old apartment. The porch was pitch-black. I couldn't look at my husband or in his direction. Tears were streaming down my face and I felt awful. I didn't want any parts of this and I felt as though I should have done something to warn Saheed. I was worried about Ryir and I felt Clarence would kill my son. He wasn't his blood and if he could kill me, what would stop him from taking out my son?

Within seconds of me standing by the payphone, Saheed pulled up. Saheed looked at my face and without me saying a word, he knew something was wrong. I stared at his face trying to tell him to leave but my lips wouldn't open. Clarence dived off the porch and... POP, POP, POP, POP, POP! He had shot Saheed five times. I screamed to the top of my lungs while Saheed darted towards his car and pulled off. I screamed louder as Clarence ran away. I stood at the phone booth screaming. Clarence had shot Saheed. I had gotten my friend involved in my hell and I didn't do anything to stop it.

The reality that my son was all alone in the house had hit me, along with the thought that Clarence was probably on his way there. I had to get back to my son. I ran as fast as I could to get around the corner, as I heard the approaching police sirens in the background. When I got back to the apartment Clarence was standing in the apartment door yelling, "Hurry the h**l up and get in here!"

I ran upstairs to check on Ryir and he was asleep. I got on my knees and prayed to God. I begged him to allow Saheed to be okay. I begged for him to keep him alive. I also asked him to forgive me for my sins and the vital role I played in this mess. A part of me wanted to believe that Clarence was not going to shoot Saheed, but I should have known better. Clarence always said he would kill me if I tried to leave him. He was capable of doing worse. I regretted the fact I had let Saheed get shot. I should have warned him and just let Clarence kill me instead. I could not believe this was my life. How had I gotten here?

For the next week I was isolated from the world. I was still off of work because of my black eyes. I did not go outside or answer the phone. Clarence watched my every move. The shooting was never discussed nor was it even mentioned. The only person who left the house was Clarence, because he continued to sell his drugs at night. He did go to the store for us and he ran errands for me because he did not want me outside. Ryir missed a week of daycare but Clarence did not care. He thought if I left the house I was going to go straight to the cops.

After a week passed, Clarence gave me permission to ride the train and take Ryir to daycare. I quickly made breakfast and Ryir and I got dressed. When we went outside I bent down to tie his sneakers. I looked up and there was a green Ford Taurus double parked in the street. Inside of the car were two white men and I knew they were detectives. I was happy to see them. They got out of their car and asked me if I was Rayna Norris. Through my tears I said "yes," and they told me to get in the car.

When we got inside of their car they told me they were investigating the shooting of Saheed. They asked me if Clarence was in the apartment and I told them he was. They called for backup and five police cars arrived on the scene. They went into the apartment while Ryir and I waited in the car. When they came out without Clarence, my heart sank. I wanted him to get caught so this disaster could be over. The detectives said they had asked the woman that lived below us if she had seen Clarence, but she told them no. I later found out that she not only lied, but that she had let Clarence out of the back door. She was on drugs and Clarence was her supplier, so she was willing to help him escape-and she did.

Ryir and I were taken to the police station. I was questioned for hours. During this time they took pictures of my eyes and I told them about the abuse, and what had led up to the shooting of Saheed. They believed me because I had confirmed what Saheed had already told them. By the grace of God I was not arrested. The detectives said that Saheed had been shot in his arm and in the chest. Words could never explain the way I felt when I heard about Saheed's injuries. I had played a part in this man being wounded when all he wanted to do was help me. I hated myself.

When the detectives told me I was free to go I returned back to the apartment. It was destroyed. The police had ransacked it while looking for Clarence and his gun. I didn't want to live there anymore. I knew Clarence would come back and kill me if I did. I went outside and sat on the steps as I tried to figure out my next move. I could barely think straight and all of a sudden I noticed a familiar car pulling up.

Clarence's mother parked and walked over towards me. She asked me what I had told the police and I lied and said nothing. She also told me that Clarence's little cousin had been murdered but because of what was going on he could not attend the funeral. The way this woman was staring at me made it clear she blamed me for everything that was going on. It was as if she was just as crazy as her son, but I didn't care what she thought about me. I wanted to be done with Clarence and everything and anyone that was connected to him. She further added how she thought it was a good idea for me to move out.

As soon as his mother pulled off I called Toya and told her what had happened. I asked her if I could stay with her until I saved up enough money to move. She said yes. I packed up our things and we went to stay with my sister.

Chapter 6
Tribulations

A few days after being picked up by the detectives, I was back on the el-train headed to work. When I stepped on the train I got a weird vibe that something wasn't right. When I sat down in my seat I heard a man seated behind me saying, "That is her." As soon as I heard his voice I knew it was Saheed. He was sitting with a woman telling her what happened. I turned around and began to cry.

His arm was in a sling and chest was wrapped in bandages. I felt terrible. He yelled out, "This is all your fault!" I tried to apologize to him but he didn't want to hear me. I tried to explain to him that Clarence threatened to kill me and my son, but he did not care. "I lost my job and I might never fully recover," he screamed. I sunk into my seat, unable to move, and I cried to no end.

After that train ride I felt horrible. I had destroyed this man's life. What made matters even worse I kept thinking about the multiple times I had left Clarence, but I always went back. If I had just stayed away from this man none of this would have happened to Saheed. I made up my mind this time would be the final time. I was never going back.

While living with Toya I started to receive counseling at the Lutheran Settlement House, Bilingual Domestic Violence Program. I talked about everything I had gone through with Clarence and I learned that I was not alone. Before I believed that only I could be living these horrors but through counseling I saw that many women and men experienced domestic violence. My counselor helped me to understand it was not my fault that I was being abused. The counselor also put the shooting of Saheed into perspective; helping me to stop blaming myself and to understand the Clarence had been the one at fault. Still it took a while for me to believe the shooting wasn't my fault. I blamed myself and often times I thought about what I could have done to save Saheed from those bullets.

Even with counseling I was extremely depressed and I had lost more weight. Although I was not with Clarence I was still living in fear. I looked over my shoulders everywhere I went. I thought he had hired someone to find and kill me because I remembered what the detectives said. They told me once they found him I'd have to come to court and testify against him. I kept feeling like there was no way I was going to do that. I tried to tell detectives how much I feared him but they said I'd have to find the courage to testify. "He shot your friend in cold blood and would have killed you and your son. You have to testify," is what one of the detectives said. I was always worried. I didn't feel safe anywhere, not even at Toya's. Clarence knew where she lived at and I kept thinking he would come there and hurt me.

During one of my counseling sessions I told my counselor about my fears and she said the agency would give me money to relocate; all I had to do was find an apartment. I looked in the newspapers and I asked my coworkers about potential places, but I didn't find anything. I no longer wanted live in West Philly because I wanted to be as far away from Clarence as I could.

After work one day I traveled to the Olney section of the city to get a neighborhood paper. I wanted to live in northwest Philadelphia. While I walked in and out of stores, looking for a paper, I saw a man who looked to be in his early forties. I asked him if he knew where I could find a neighborhood paper but he didn't. Then, without realizing what was happening, I asked if he knew anyone who was renting apartments and he said he did. He gave me his friend's name and number. Two weeks later I moved into that man's friend's apartment. God had blessed me yet again.

The apartment was located on Cliveden Street in Germantown. It was on the second floor of the building and the front door could not be opened without a key. These two amenities made me feel a little safer. My counselor had given me a cell phone that was equipped to call the police with just a stroke of a button. Although these things put me at ease I was still very fearful that Clarence would find me and kill me.

The most mind blowing factor of it all was that through my fears, I still loved Clarence. Through counseling I learned that my feelings were normal because I was in love with the part of Clarence that was not abusive. I held on to the way he treated me when things where good. I loved the way he treated my children; even though it was clear they were being affected by the abuse they had heard and witnessed. All of the feelings I had were confusing and it drove me insane. It was as if I was still allowing Clarence to control my life even though he was not around.

Once we were settled into our apartment I tried to get my life back in order. I continued to get Ryan on the weekends and tried to build a stronger, more secure relationship with my boys. I continued to work and I was offered a position as an assistant manager. I took it and I began to thrive at my job. I had a good reputation with my bosses, and those who worked for me respected and enjoyed being on my shift. No one at my job ever knew the things I had gone through and I wanted to remain professional and grow as much as I could within the company.

As I continued to pick up the pieces of my life and to rebuild, out of nowhere I received a phone call that threw me off my square. The detectives told me that they had caught him. I became physically sick. I knew I would have to face him in court. How could I face him? I couldn't. I was so scared.

I panicked. Everywhere I went I was filled with fear. I was afraid on the bus, at work, and even in my apartment. I thought every man that passed me in the street was a hired hit-man, who had been sent by Clarence to end my life. I avoided all male shoppers at work. When a male customer came in the store, I waited in the stockroom until they left, before returning to the floor. I was driving myself crazy. In order to release the anxiety of my thoughts, I visited him in prison. I thought if I could just ask him if he had hired someone to kill me, he would tell me the truth. It had been several months since I had last seen him, and when I did I barely recognized him. He grew out his hair and had a full beard.

The sight of him instantly reminded me of all the things he had done to me. However, I loved Clarence and I wanted him to love me too; the way he did when we first met. He was surprised and happy to see me. Again he apologized for all of the things he had done to me. He said he was getting counseling and it was teaching him how to control his anger. He said he was learning how to rebuild himself so he could be a good husband to me. He assured me no one was following me and that he would never hire anyone to kill me.

I loosened up. I told him about my promotion and my new place. He said he was proud of me. I asked him for proof that he was going to counseling and he said once he got home he would show me the certificate of completion. I believed everything he said. I believed that my fairy tale was capable of coming true and when he asked me not to come to court, I agreed. Right before my visit ended he told me to kiss the boys for him, and it was then time for me to go.

I continued to visit him the entire time he was in prison. We talked about the things he learned in counseling and I was happy for him. I was excited at the idea I could get Clarence back; the man I had met two years prior to the abuse.

Unexpectedly the case against Clarence was dropped because Saheed failed to go to court. I later found out that Clarence's family had contacted Saheed and paid him not to testify. Clarence was never convicted of shooting Saheed.

When Clarence came home we were one big happy family. He went out and bought me a new wedding ring and he said it represented our new beginning. He also bought me a car. We started to do the things we did when we first met. We took the kids out and did things as a family. He treated me better than he had ever done before. He moved into my apartment and helped me with the bills and the children. I believed that Clarence had finally changed but I still wanted a little proof. When I asked him for the certificate verifying his completion of his anger management class, he said it got lost in his paperwork. Once again I believed him.

For a few weeks Clarence was the perfect man. Clarence was like a drug and I was addicted to him. I was addicted to the way he treated me when things were good. I was addicted to the way he showed love to my children. I was addicted to the things he did for me. I thought I loved him but I soon discovered that I did not love myself...and that some things about Clarence would never change.

Like clockwork he was back to his old self again. He began to question me about the things that I did while he was away in prison. Clarence taunted me and accused me of being a whore. He said he knew I had slept with multiple men while he was locked up. I had no time to see anyone and I was so fearful of someone taking my life, that meeting anyone new was the last of my concerns. I tried to convince him but he did not believe me. Immediately I began regretting allowing him back into my life. He had not changed at all.

He destroyed my apartment as he looked for evidence of me cheating. His search for proof quickly turned into him physically abusing me again when he found an encouragement card. It was from a male friend of mine that helped me move into my apartment. I explained to him that the card was innocent but he punched my back like a punching bag; ignoring everything I was saying. When he finally got tired of punching my back, he then beat it with a hard wooden hair brush. My entire back was covered with black and blue open sores. I tried to put my shirt on but he wouldn't allow it, as he threw rubbing alcohol all over my back. I screamed and begged for mercy. I promised him I would be the perfect wife and do everything he wanted me to do if he would just stop pouring the alcohol on my back. At some point he finally stopped.

Later that day we went to his mother's house and he told her about the card. He never told her that it was a friendly gesture from a friend who wanted to encourage me on my new move. He got upset all over again and pushed me down to the ground. When I hit the floor he began to stomp me, thrashing my entire body with his hard boots. He did all of this right in front of his mother. Her reaction was unpredictable as she calmly watched and said, "You shouldn't do that to her." Again I regretted staying with him as I balled up on the floor and tried to protect myself. He looked at his mother and said, "It's her fault! Nobody told her to take no d**n cards from no man! If she was a good wife I wouldn't have to beat her!"

The next day when I went to work one of my coworkers placed her hand on my back while we were talking. I screamed at Denise because it hurt so badly. She knew I was being abused because I had shared my dark secret with her while Clarence was jailed. She was supportive to me and a good friend to talk to. When I showed her my back she could not believe what he had done to me. Further, she couldn't understand why I stayed. I tried to explain my reasoning but she didn't want to hear it; and truthfully at that point I didn't want to either. No reason or excuse I could think of would make any sense for as to why I stayed with a man who was bent on one day killing me.

Clarence was back to his old ways. He began accusing me of sleeping with people in the neighborhood, which was silly because I did not know anyone there. One day while driving home from an outing he accused me of sleeping with a man that lived around the corner from my apartment. I had no idea who he was talking about. While stopped at a stop sign he said that I was staring at the house that the man lived in. Without warning he slapped me in the face.

When we got home I started to fold clothes while Ryir watched television. I knew the fight wasn't over because he had convinced himself that I was sleeping with this neighbor. He kept staring at me and I was scared. He got off the couch and pushed me on the floor. When I hit the floor I tried my best not to cry out. I didn't want Ryir to hear me cry or to watch Clarence beat me for the millionth time. I felt terrible because while Clarence was in jail my children and I were happy. No abuse, no drama, just love and appreciation towards and for one another;

now this.

After hitting the floor he grabbed me by my right breast. His nails where embedded under my breast. By far this was the worse pain I had ever felt but it didn't stop him. He dragged me into the bedroom as I begged him to leave me alone but of course he wouldn't.

"Tell me the truth," he screamed as he questioned me about my neighbor. I pleaded with him to realize I had been telling the truth. I told him that he was acting irrational because I was new to the neighborhood and didn't know anybody. I was frustrated and tired, as my words fell on deaf ears. I yelled out, "I just want to die! I'm tired! I just want to kill myself!" I pulled the window up and I went to leap out of it, but Clarence hit me in the back of my head with that wooden hair brush and stopped me. I wanted it to end but he pulled me back into his world. The hickey on the back of my head began to throb and it wouldn't take long for it to swell up to the size of a small grapefruit. Clarence didn't care. He said, "I'll hit you again if you ever try to kill yourself! You stupid b***h!"

His words meant nothing to me. I was tired. I was sick of being accused and beaten. I grabbed Ryir by the hand and ran out of the apartment. I didn't know where I was going but I did not want to be with him anymore. Clarence ran out behind us and got into his car. When we ran around the corner Clarence was fast on our trail. He drove his car on the pavement and almost hit us. The car was so close to our bodies that I could feel the heat from the exhaust pipe, but I wasn't giving up. We were able to squeeze by the car and we continued running. Ryir and I were both screaming and crying.

When we reached the middle of the street I heard a car's horn. We ran faster because I thought it was Clarence. Then a female called out my name. I looked up and it was David's cousin, Tina. She yelled, "Get in the car. Come on!" We jumped into her vehicle and I started to tell her what had happened, as I tried to hold back my tears. She said, "I knew something was going on because David had..." Before she could finish telling me that David had told her about the abuse, Clarence crashed into the back of her car. I couldn't speak. Why was he crashing into the back of her car? This man was crazy. I begged Tina not to stop driving. I screamed at her to keep going. She started to scream at Clarence because he continued to rear end her. I begged her not to stop the car. I did not want him to hurt us. She tried to drive away but he was on her tail. Eventually she pulled over and said, "You have to get out! He's ruining my new car and he's going to kill all of us! Rayna, I'm sorry."

We got out but I was not giving up. I started to run again. I heard another horn beep and again I was afraid. But this time it was a woman that had been driving on the same street as us and she told us to get into her car. Without hesitation we did. She said everything was going to be okay. I did not know if it would be or not. I only knew I didn't want him to get us.

Once in this woman's car I did not see Clarence anymore. She took us to her house and I told her what was going on. This stranger shared with me her past experience of abuse and gave me a glimpse of hope that I would live again. She was a very sweet older woman. She gave us something to eat and drink, and then she took us to Toya's house.

For a few days we stayed at Toya's house. When I went back to my apartment I prayed that Clarence was not there. I was tired and did not want to be with him anymore. I was tired of being tired. When I put my key into the door I got an eerie feeling and I knew that something was wrong. Slowly I opened the door and I could not believe what I saw.

There was black writing on my ceiling that read "I AM NOT CRAZY YOU ARE!!!" My leather couches, that

I had purchased several months prior, had rips and slits all over them. There were feathers all over the room. My shoes were in bags on the living room floor and my closets and drawers were empty. My glass vanity was knocked over and broken glass was scattered all over the floor. I looked all over the apartment for my clothes but they were nowhere to be found. He had gotten rid of all of my clothes, including all my bras and panties .I knew I had left my debit card in the apartment when I ran out, and that was missing also. I sat on the floor and cried. This man had ruined my life. Everything that I had worked so hard for had been destroyed.

Every first Saturday of the month my landlord would come to my apartment to collect his rent and to exterminate. It was early in the week so I only had a few days to get the apartment back in order. The writing on the ceiling was done with a lighter. I took a piece of the paint chip and went to Home Depot. I got the matching paint so I could cover the ceiling, and when I got home I began the tedious task of painting the ceiling and cleaning up the apartment. I couldn't get anyone to move the couches so I covered them with sheets when the landlord came.

Later that week the couches had to be sawed down, just to remove them from the apartment and to place them out with my trash. With the help of several people I was able to slowly regain a wardrobe. Ryan's grandmother bought me underwear, Mena bought me clothes, and others gave me what they could. I had support and it felt good. A few weeks had gone by and I did not speak to Clarence. I was slowly attempted to rebuild my life without him and then I was arrested.

Two o'clock in the morning my doorbell rang. I was sure that it was Clarence. When I looked out of the window there was a cop car doubled parked in the street. Two plainclothes cops were inside; a black male and female. When I got to the door the man said, "Rayna Norris?" I hesitated for a minute before saying, "Yes." He told me to open the door and they followed me back to my apartment. I thought Clarence was back in trouble and they were there to question me about him. I was used to that because of his lifestyle as a drug dealer. Once we were in my apartment I was prepared to tell them that I had not spoken to or seen Clarence, but the male detective told me that I was being arrested for robbing Jaleel Ganner at gunpoint.

I started to cry. What was he talking about? I have never robbed anyone. I told them he was mistaken but they did not believe me. They asked me if I had children in the house and I told them my son was sleeping. They said I had five minutes to get someone to pick him up or they'd call the Department of Human Services and turn him over to them. My girlfriend Gail lived around the corner so I called her and she came and took Ryir. I was handcuffed in front of my son and taken to the police station.

Once there the detectives told me that Jaleel came to the police station and reported to them that Toya and I robbed him in a white Tahoe truck. They said we pulled a gun out on him and took his chain. Jaleel had lied. There was no way this story was true but I could see the connection. Clarence had gotten Jaleel to make a false report because I was never going back to him. He probably thought that Tina or I was going to try and get him locked up because he rammed into the back of Tina's car. He wanted to destroy my life any way he could and he was using his friend to help him. I desperately explained to the police that Jaleel was my abusive husband's friend. At first they did not believe a word I was saying until I continued to tell them about the abuse I had suffered. I also told them that Ganner was not Jaleel's real last name. They wanted proof. I told them that Clarence's mother knew the truth but I wasn't sure if this woman would confess it.

While the detectives looked up Jaleel's real name, they sent the cops to Clarence's mother house to see if the information I had given them was true. After sitting in the police station for over five hours they had finally located Jaleel's true identity through the driver's license database. The cops also talked to Clarence's mother and surprisingly she told them her son had convinced his friend to make the false report. The cops picked Jaleel up and I had to point him out in a line-up. Behind the protective and opaque glass I stared at him. How could one grown man convince another grown man to make a false police report against someone who had never done anything to them? That was something I would never understand.

I had to go to court and I hated every minute of it. The one time I had to go into the courtroom I saw Jaleel but I don't know what happened to him because after that day I was never required to return. I was cleared of the accusations and no charges were placed on my record. It would be just a few weeks after the incident with Jaleel that Clarence would return into my life.

He talked his way back in. He promised to treat me better and to get help. I was afraid if I didn't take him back he would kill me, and I still believed that our marriage could work if I figured out what I kept doing wrong.

The cycle of violence continued. One minute we were a loving happy couple, and the next minute Clarence became outraged over the accusations he created in his mind. I was going crazy. Abuse was a part of my everyday life. It became normal to me.

One evening while Clarence slept I took a hammer and thought about hitting him in the head with it. I felt myself becoming very angry and I wanted my revenge. I found myself becoming a different person; someone who was filled with rage. I did not feel like myself anymore. I wanted to abuse Clarence. Instead of asking Clarence to stop hitting me, I would now demand it. That night I did not hit Clarence but it was not to long after that when my anger and rage would spill out.

One morning while dropping Ryir off at pre-school, the school maintenance man was walking in the building the same time as I. He said good morning to me but I didn't speak back. I knew Clarence was watching me. I walked in the building with my head down, just like I always did, and kept my mouth shut. When I got back into the car Clarence drove off. He started to accuse me of being disrespectful and said I had spoken to the maintenance man. He then accused me of sleeping with him. When I denied his accusations he stopped the car and punched me in the mouth. Blood went everywhere. My lips immediately swelled up and I was livid. Rage filled my body and I reminded Clarence to stop hitting me. He laughed and said, "You just keep making me hit you."

While Clarence drove down the street I picked up the club (a car security device) that was on the passenger side floor. I separated the top of the club from the bottom, so I could have a better grip on it and I began to beat Clarence in the top of his head with it. I could not stop hitting him. I used all the force I had in my body and I hit him harder with each blow I struck. I don't know what came over me. In that moment I hated him and I hated the fact that he thought I was his personal punching bag. He begged me to stop but I couldn't. It took us almost crashing into the back of a house before I stopped.

Seeing Clarence hurting, in pain, vulnerable and weak, I realized that he bled the same way that I did. I also realized that I could hurt him just like he had hurt me. That day I made up my mind that he was just a man and I was never going to be scared of him again. God created us equally and the only one I would fear was God.

When we got back to the apartment I was bleeding from my mouth, but Clarence had over a dozen hickeys on his head. Clarence suffered from severe migraines and usually I'd be trying to nurse any wounds he suffered. Now not only did I enjoy seeing the bruises I had placed on him, but I relished in the agony they caused him. The loving and caring wife he had abused was no longer available; she had gone. I had changed. After that incident I was numb and had become someone I did not like.

Clarence's physical abuse now shifted to severe verbal abuse. He had always been verbally abusive but now it escalated. He knew that I was no longer afraid of him so he didn't bother putting his hands on me but his mouth was nasty. The things that he began to say to me cut through my heart. Instead of calling me by my name he'd call me a whore, slut, a b***h, a cunt; and of course he accused me of sleeping around. He told me that I would never be anything and I came from nothing. He said I wasn't a good mother and that's why David had taken my son from me. He said if Ryir's father was home he would have come for his son too. Clarence laughed when I asked why he would speak to his wife the way he did. He said, "You're not my wife. You're just someone I have sex with and hang out with when I'm bored." I wondered how anything offensive he said could hurt me when I had taken a stand against the physical abuse, but words cut deep. They are often harsher than a punch or a slap to the face.

I had no self-esteem or self-worth. I didn't respond to his attacks and did not argue with him. I was just there; moving around but not truly present. I believe one day Clarence finally got tired of the relationship, or lack of one, and he moved out. His mother and I cosigned for him to get his own apartment in West Philly. Although we were married we agreed it was best for him to move out. He still visited me or spied on me whenever he wanted to.

During one of his visits we got into an argument. He came charging at me as if he was going to punch me and the new Rayna was ready. I started to throw picture frames at him and I was looking for anything I could grab and attack him with. The kids were screaming for me to stop but I refused to stand there and let him hit me. Clarence also begged me to stop throwing things at him, but I kept on. He then began to throw the picture frames back at me. That pissed me off even more because I told him not to hit me again. I took an iron and wrapped the cord around my wrist; just enough to have room to sling it at him and pull it back. As he began to walk closer to me I started to hit him with the iron. He screamed and told me to stop because he wasn't going to hit me. I didn't believe him so I continued to hit him. He left the apartment as I continued to fling the iron at him until the door was closed.

I talked to the kids and apologized to them. I had said sorry so many times that I was sure they were tired of hearing me. I started to clean the apartment up so I could put the children to bed. As soon as I laid the kids down the electricity went out. I had paid my electricity bill and it was too late in the evening for my service to be interrupted. I wasn't sure what was going on. I went to the window and I saw Clarence pull off in his car. He had pulled the electric box off the back of my building and our power was off. I guess he thought since he had lost that fight he needed to do something to get me back. But I wasn't defeated. I called the electric company and they came out that night and replaced the box.

However, I did eventually lose the battle to stay in my apartment because of my husband's foolishness. Clarence had done so much destruction that I could not repair it all. There were holes in the walls, the doors were damaged, and I could not afford to get all of the damages repaired. My neighbors complained to my landlord about the constant fights and they were tired of being disturbed with our nonsense. Because I was afraid that I would be evicted, Ryir and I moved in with Clarence in his efficiency apartment.

The verbal abuse continued and for me it was worse than the physical abuse I had endured. The bruises from his physical abuse would heal but the words he spoke to me just stuck with me. My fear for Clarence was diminishing but my hate for him grew. On a Saturday afternoon I had to work and Clarence agreed to watch Ryir. He brought Ryir to my job and accused me of sleeping with the security guard. He got upset and left the store, but he didn't take Ryir with him. I kept calling his phone but he did not answer. I was the only manager on duty and I needed to be attentive and on my job. Without anyone to watch my son, I left the store and placed the stock associate in charge.

As I was walking to the train Clarence was waiting. I attempted to walk past him but he took his arm and struck me in the neck. The force caused me to hit the floor. I got up and at the moment I was done. It was time for me to leave and to never look back. I was tired and my children were tired. I had broken so many promises to them and I had failed them. I had been stupid and I was tired of hearing all the excuses that I had made up to stay. I was tired of forgiving a man that would never appreciate me, who'd never know who I was and see my beauty. I was tired of the rage that brewed in me. Tired of the bruises and the verbal abuse he continued to lash upon me. I was tired of feeling as if I could never be good enough. I was done. I was tired. I was finished and nothing and no one would change my mind this time. If I did not leave this time one of us would end up in jail; because if he did not kill me I was ready to put an end to his life.

I went back to the apartment and called Ashley,

Aunt Shingie's daughter. I knew she had her own place and I needed somewhere to stay. I asked her if I could live with her for about a month until I found my own place and she said yes. I packed up our things while Clarence watched. He took my eye glasses, pocketbooks, clothes, my wedding ring, and other things he had purchased me. I didn't care. Those material things had no value to me. They could all be bought again but my life, that's what I wanted back. There could be no more bargaining on my happiness. I wanted out for good.

Ryir and I moved to Germantown with Ashley. I told her that I would buy food for the house but I needed to save the rest of my money so I could move out. She was very understanding and agreed to those terms. I changed Ryir's school, worked hard, and began to look for another apartment.

While talking to Ashley one day I told her about the many things I had gone through with Clarence. She brought up a childhood experience when I saw my Aunt Shingie. She asked me why of all my family members had Aunt Shingie chosen to visit me. I really didn't know and the more I thought about it, I just did not have an answer. When I went to tell her that I was clueless, the Holy Spirit spoke to me. It was clear that my aunt's fate could have been my own. I was experiencing the same abuse she had gone through and still did not take heed to the many warnings that had been set before my eyes. My own aunt had been killed by her abusive partner at just twenty-six years of age. She had two children, just like I had, and he killed her. What made me any different? Why hadn't I seen Aunt Shingie in me? I was twenty-six and going through the exact same things that Aunt Shingie had suffered. God revealed to me that my fate would be no different if I did not leave Clarence for good. It was now clear to me why I had seen Aunt Shingie. It had all became clear what she was trying to tell me.

Thirty days after I moved in with Ashley I found a new apartment. It was a two bedroom located on the corner of 16th Street and Olney Avenue. I started the rebuilding process but there were parts of me that just didn't seem to die. I had my epiphany moment when I spoke to Ashley. I had been tired and I was sure I would never go back to a life of pain; but my feelings for Clarence would not leave me. During this time I had stopped counseling. I began to restore my relationships with my friends and family...but I could not tell them that I was secretly seeing Clarence.

He knew where I lived but I didn't allow him into my home. I would go to his apartment or sometimes we'd go out. I knew in my heart I had to end it with Clarence permanently. I could never respect myself for dealing with him. What could I tell my children whom I had let down so many times? What else could be said to my friends despite the fact that I was clearly stupid? He was an addiction that was so overpowering that only God could deliver me.

I sat in the living room of my apartment one day and I opened up. I could hide no longer. My heart was heavy and my soul was in need of healing. I was tired of being disobedient and I finally whole heartedly leaned on God for his help and his healing. I cried out to my Father. I told him that without him I would never leave the clutches of the hell I lived in. I knew I would die if he would not come into my life and free my mind, body, and soul from the abuse. I needed God to save me so I would never go back to Clarence again. I cried, I screamed, and I prayed to be released. Whatever hold Clarence had on me I begged my Father to set me free.

Chapter 7
Glory

September of 2004, Duke came home from prison; which was only one month after I had moved into my apartment. He came to visit me the day he got out and we started talking. We talked about his time in prison and the things that I had gone through with Clarence. For the first time ever I told him that I had married Clarence, and it was clear that information truly hurt him. He knew I was being abused but he never knew I had gotten married. I was embarrassed. Not because I was married but at the type of marriage I had. I also was finally able to talk to him about the hit men that Clarence said wanted Duke, Ryir, and myself dead. Duke didn't even know Clarence, and once he said that I was sure the rest of his story about the hit men was false. Clarence had used Duke's street credibility as a pawn and a scare tactic; and it had worked on me.

While crying in each other's arms, one thing led to another and we had sex. My emotions overcame me and even though I was going through many things with Clarence, I felt bad because under God's law I was still a married woman. I prayed and asked God for forgiveness.

A few weeks after Duke had been home I missed

my menstrual cycle. I took a pregnancy test and I was pregnant. Duke and I had only slept together once but I knew it wasn't Clarence's baby because he was sterile and couldn't have children. I contemplated an abortion and I even made an appointment. The day that I was scheduled to go to the clinic I called Duke and told him I was pregnant. He was upset with me because he had seen me talking to Clarence a few days prior. It was so much going on and I was confused about all the different emotions I was feelings. I told him that I was scheduled to get an abortion that evening. He was against it. He said he wanted his baby. I was full of shame. I was pregnant by Duke but married to Clarence. And despite the things Clarence put me through I didn't want to dishonor our marriage by having a baby by another man.

I went to the abortion clinic and sat down and waited for my name to be called. I sat there and looked around and asked myself why I was there. I had no reason to be there and this baby is what I had prayed for. I asked God to do something so that I would never go back to Clarence. God had answered my prayers. He may have not done it the way I thought he was going to, but he had blessed me with life and a way out. The baby I was carrying inside of my stomach would save my life.

After I made the decision to keep my baby I was through with Clarence. I know the act of having sex with Duke was a sin but the baby I was carrying was not. God does not make mistakes and he alone creates life. He created my baby to save me and nine months later on Ryan's birthday, I gave birth to my third son Rymir; the baby that God sent to save my life.

I never went back to Clarence after I found out I was pregnant. I didn't see him again until I served him with the final divorce papers, which was in October of 2006. He made me wait two years before he would sign. I had been with Clarence from September 2001, until September 2004, and although it felt as if my life was going to end, it hadn't.

After the relationship with Clarence resolved, my life began to focus around the person who mattered most, which was me. Duke and I started a relationship. It was tough being in another relationship because of what I had been through, but Duke stood by me. I brought my baggage and I was for the moment, damaged goods; but Duke never gave up on me. He often wondered what had happened to the person he knew before he went to prison. He feared that he'd never fully see her again. The truth was she was gone. The naïve Rayna had changed but I was not destroyed.

I went back to church. I attended the Liberty Bible Christian Fellowship with the kids in West Philly. I had to rebuild my broken relationship with Christ. Although I had abandoned our relationship I knew that he had never left me. I was welcomed back with open arms and I thanked God for his mercy. I prayed often and I studied my bible. I did my best to live my life according to the word.

A friend of mine that I met through work named Victoria began to go to church with me. Even though I was already a member of Liberty, I never attended my new member's classes. When Victoria joined the church I completed my classes with her. I learned a lot about myself and my relationship with God grew stronger. I began to question my purpose in life and the path that God had chosen for me. I grew unhappy with my work because I knew it was not in line with what God wanted for me. Victoria made a random suggestion that I go to college. I was twenty-eight and in my head I was too old to go back to school. She thought I was crazy for letting my age stop me from pursing a purposeful career that could assist me with my calling.

The day we graduated from new member's class, Bishop Fuller preached about pursuing dreams and how fear holds people back from their full potential. He talked about going to school and allowing God to move in your life. While he was preaching, Victoria kept glaring and smiling at me because she knew this word was especially for me. That message changed my life. I started to think about my purpose in a different way. I did not know what it was but I knew that school would take me one step closer to finding it.

One afternoon I stood in my living room and prayed. Well in all honestly it seemed like I was having a screaming competition with my maker. I told God that if he wanted me to attend school, then he would have to tell me clearly. If it was his plan he had to take over the process. I knew my fear would not allow me to do this on my own, but if it was the will of God it would be done.

A few weeks later there was an advertisement on the radio about Eastern in The City (EIC), a Christian School of Social Change that offered and off-site two year program. They were having an open house for their inner city campus, located in the Spring Garden section of Philadelphia. The advertisement caught my attention so I attended.

During the open house I learned they were providing scholarships and laptop computers for those that attended. The school would assist with the application process and financial aid assistance. The thing that I loved most about the school was the student's age diversity. There were students my age, younger, and older, who were applying to the school. I stepped out on faith and applied even though I had never taken my SAT's and hadn't been in school for over nine years.

A few weeks later I received an acceptance letter. God is good! I had no idea what to major in because I still did not know what God wanted me to do. I began to read through the catalog. Some years prior I was prophesied to about being a teacher and I took that to mean it in the tradition sense. Still I was not sure what major was right for me. I prayed and asked God for direction.

Eastern in The City was a two year program; and the students had an option to transfer to the main campus after completion of the program to obtain a Bachelor's degree. The staff at EIC took the students on a bus trip to the main campus for a tour. On the ride there I was reading over a course description manual. While reading the narrative for education I knew that was not what God wanted me to do. I continued to read through the book and silently prayed for clarity. Suddenly I came across the social work major. While reading it that lovely voice spoke to me and said "This is it." Every word of the description screamed out to me, "This is you! This is what you are supposed to be doing!" I gave God thanks and when it was time I declared social work as my major.

The next four years was tough. College was very challenging but through God and with my strength and determination to please him, I succeeded. By the time I graduated from college in 2010, Duke and I were married. I had purchased my first house, my second car, and my fourth son Rylei was born. God moved in my life in a mighty way. The road was rough but God prevailed. He told me through my social work degree my concentration and focus would be on Domestic Violence. Through prayer God revealed to me the reason I went through the abuse with Clarence. It was only to help other woman like myself. I did not go through that torment just to declare that I was a domestic violence survivor. By no means am I the poster child for domestic violence. However, I am the poster child for the things that God can do in someone's life.

After graduating from Eastern University with a 3.4 Grade Point Average and a Bachelor of Social Work,

I became a Family Advocate for Lutheran Settlement House's Bilingual Domestic Violence Program. I empower women through case management to change their lives. God enabled me to have a long standing relationship with LSH. Not only was I a client, I became a volunteer, and I completed my internship with them too. God places people in your life for a reason. I truly believe that everything we go through is to bless someone else. I do not regret any trials or tribulations that I went through because it made me the person that I am today.

During all of my adult life I searched for my father. The time I felt like I needed him most was when I was in the abusive relationship with Clarence. I thought my father would save me from all the evil in this world but that never happened. In January 2011, I received a friend request on Facebook from a Maya Dixon. I knew from her last name that she was a family member on my father's side. I quickly accepted her friend request and we exchanged phone numbers. I was so excited I could barely contain myself. I shared with my husband Duke that my family member had found me on Facebook, and that I was finally going too reconnected with my father. I was so happy and he was happy for me as well. Although I had not spoken to my dad in fifteen years I still loved him, and I couldn't wait to hear his voice.

During my lunch break at work I decided to call Maya. After several rings she answered. I tried to remain calm and listen to her while she told me about my family who lived in Philadelphia and in Atlanta. I did not want to be rude and cut her off, but I did not want to hear about them. I wanted to talk with my dad. I started to ask about him but before I could get my question out, she delivered the worst news I had ever heard in my entire life. My father had been found dead in his Tennessee apartment just one week before I had called her. He had suffered a massive heart attack and it had been several days before anyone found him.

My world came crashing down. I waited a long time to see my dad. Connecting with her on Facebook was the connection I needed to tell my dad how much I loved and missed him. Now it was clear that would never happen.

My family did not want to have a service for him until they found me. She assured me that my father was looking for me too, but due to lack of education and his limited technical abilities, it was almost impossible for him to locate me. We said our goodbyes and we hung up. I instantly became weak and started to cry hysterically. How could this be true? I was angry. If she had contacted me why didn't anyone help my father reach out to me before he died? I just wanted to tell my father I loved him. I knew he had always loved me and I felt horrible that I'd never get to see or hear from him again.

My father's ashes arrived a week later and we had a memorial service for him. I reconnected with my paternal side of the family and although that was great, I would have traded them all in if I could have just reconnected with my dad. I know everything happens for a reason and a part of me wants to believe that God kept my father away from me because he would have went to prison for killing Clarence. My father had a history of hurting those that hurt his family. He had even served prison time behind it. This may not be the reason my father was not in my life but I do know there is a reason. God just didn't reveal it to me yet.

Today I have a healthy and prospering relationship with Toya. My sister and I have ironed out our differences. She confessed to me that she was angered when I was born. She had wanted to be the only girl child and when my mother had me she was not pleased. Once we became adults she apologized for the way she had treated me when I stayed with her. It was a good feeling to clear up those past wounds and we continue to build our bond. My biological mother has been clean from abusing drugs for over six years. I am very proud of her and our relationship is a work in progress. My mom, my Aunt Deborah, we are still close. She has never turned her back on me and I'm amazed at how much love we share for one another. I can talk to her and she gets me. She's a blessing and I'm forever thankful to God for placing her in my life.

My marriage with Duke grows strong every day. He is my rock and I love him for loving me just the way I am. I am enough for him. He supports me and he always shows me love. I have custody of Ryan! Together Duke and I have five beautiful children, who we love and adore. Ryir had to receive counseling and therapy for the abuse that he witnessed, but he is doing well. He is an honor roll student that will make a mark on this world regardless of the tragedies he has seen.

Clarence, yes I did see him again. When the book was finished I was driving in my car and I pulled up next to him. I looked in his direction and he had a female passenger with him. She was in the same position that I used to sit in. Her head was down and she had a look of fear on her face. The light changed and without him noticing me, he turned and life moved on. I felt no anger. I felt no fear; only freedom from a way of life that could only end badly.

God has changed my life forever and I am grateful for the path that I am now on. I know that the field of domestic violence is a part of my calling but it is not all I have been called upon to do. I am a mother, a wife, a sister, a friend, a believer, a survivor, a counselor, an author, and the rest...well I'm still a work in progress!

My Message To You...

God never allowed anything to happen to me that I could not handle or that he did not bring me through. I am a testimony and if going through some tough times will allow me to help someone else, why not me?

I did not write this book because I wanted to. I wrote this book because this is what God wanted me to do. Before every writing session I prayed and asked him to help me put these words on paper. I wanted his full control over this project.

But fear almost caused me not to write this book. Fear of what people might say, fear of the unknown, and the fear of hurting people I care for almost kept me from serving my purpose. Fear had a hold on me but thankfully God had a stronger grip.

We often hold ourselves back from our full potential, and from living in tune with God's purpose for us. I will do my best to keep fear at bay. I will also be obedient so that on that Day of Judgment God can say to me, "Well done good and faithful servant. Well done."

There Is Help:

If you or anyone you know has been physically, verbally, or sexually abused, please call the:

National Domestic Abuse Hotline
1(800) 799- SAFE

This work is a memoir. It reflects the memory of the author's experiences. Some names have been changed in order to protect their privacy.

To order additional copies of

7:17

please contact:
Arnaz Publishing
5220 Whitby Avenue
Philadelphia, PA. 19143
(215) 474-2717